NOV 16 1986 pd

DATE DUE

American Poetry
in the
Twentieth Century

American Poetry
in the
Twentieth Century

Kenneth Rexroth

Herder and Herder

1971
HERDER AND HERDER NEW YORK
232 Madison Avenue, New York 10016

Library of Congress Catalog Card Number: 76–150308
© 1971 by Herder and Herder, Inc.
Manufactured in the United States

To My Friend
JAMES LAUGHLIN
to whom modern literature
owes an incalculable debt

American Poetry
in the
Twentieth Century

I.

THE long-term tendencies in American poetry reflect the major influences that went to form the culture as a whole and these in turn the ethnic and national groups who have made up the American people.

First in point of time of course was the American Indian, and the Indian endures as subtle, all-pervasive background, both in vestiges of Indian cultural contributions in a positive sense, and in reverse, as the sense of guilt which haunts American history. At no time except at the very beginning has there not been somewhere, on the part of some poet, an attempt to incorporate directly the Indian heritage. Equally important to the traditionally raised children of older families, the Indians took the places of the deities of earth and air, of springs and trees and mountains. They were the satyrs and nymphs of the American child, his connection with the earth beneath his feet. People reared in our contemporary society of urban nomads, broken families, computerized education, and televised leisure can form no conception of the role played by tales of the American Indian in the older, more stable society. It is significant that after the middle of the twentieth century, as the technological empire reached its apogee, the youth revolt turned once again to the American Indian for inspiration and restoration.

Spanish influence in American literature was minimal until the settling up of the Southwest in the twentieth century—Prescott, some poems of Longfellow's—very little else. It is extraordinary that the long, heroic wars of liberation of Latin America attracted little attention in the North, so little that they made no significant impression on literature. Bolivar and Juarez were unknown to the American schoolboy. In recent years the American empire has become frightened by its relations with its Southern vassals and the history of Latin America is touched on briefly in some schools, particularly those in communities with large Latin populations. But these are "lessons," not heroic myths. Today, international writers like Octavio Paz and Gabriella Mistral may be mentioned briefly in college courses, called of all things "Chicano literature," but I doubt if one-tenth of 1 per cent of the "Spanish majors" in the schools of America have ever heard of Rubén Darío. Spanish influence in American poetry comes late, from Spain via translations of Federico García Lorca. Even specialists in Spanish translation like W. S. Merwin show no influence of Machado, Alberti, or Paz in their own poetry. Perhaps Pablo Neruda has at least set an example for some revolutionary poetry.

The English influence we are all familiar with, but only specialists realize the peculiar nature of that influence, the very odd literary sensibility produced by the ideal of the Puritan theocratic city state, an intensely baroque religiosity. There is a Protestant Baroque sensibility as eccentric as that of the Counter Reformation Catholic poet, Richard Crashaw. Anne Bradstreet, our first poet, was a disciple of Francis Quarles. Anne, remember, was welcomed by the literary establishment of the home land as "a right Du Bartas girl." Du Bartas, in case you don't know, was the most extreme metaphysical poet of his time, quite the equal of the Spaniard Góngora or the Italian Marino, but a Protestant militant, a French Huguenot. The translation from French of his poetic works by John Sylvester was a best-seller for two generations, and my copy with its beautiful title page once belonged to a New England parson.

It is simply not true that there was a continuity in the Southern colonies of a cavalier tradition. The cavalier South, as Mark Twain pointed out, is a dream of chronic adolescents who read themselves to sleep with the novels of Sir Walter Scott. The real Southern tradition was largely French, Girondin, rationalistic. Its great representative is Jefferson, but its appearance in literature is minimal south of Virginia. Its outstanding literary representative, our own *philosophe,* is in fact *le bon Franklin,* hardly a Southerner.

The second most powerful current, or *Geist,* or *Weltanschauung,* in American literature, is French—New France of the waterways and portages of the St. Lawrence, Great Lakes, and Mississippi drainages. New France was a very peculiar kind of France, and bore more resemblance to Kievan Russia with its Varangian, Kazar, and Bulgar river-borne fur traders than anything to be found in the homeland. Its forts and trading posts were communities of armed merchant adventurers. Most of the women were Indians, and later also Negroes and mixed bloods. A masculine, anarchistic, sensual culture grew up of the same character as the Cossacks', or before them, the Vikings'. No other people assimilated and were assimilated so completely, by not just Indians, Negroes, and Spanish, but by the American land. We forget that they were there before the birth of the Republic, from Pittsburgh to the Rockies and from Hudson's Bay to the Gulf. Parkman wrote fourteen volumes

11

of a history which he saw as the struggle of the anal-retentive British against the oral, sensual, sloppy French. He was right. This struggle still goes on, the Jazz Age against Anthony Comstock, the hips against the uptights. It finds its most conscious expression today in the fantasies of that voluntary Wasp, Leslie Fiedler, who finds the greatest spokesman of the riverain culture, Mark Twain, totally incomprehensible; and like all uptight people when so confronted, he can only dismiss him as a homosexual, like a policeman confronted by a student with bare feet and long hair.

To return to Ben Franklin. He was more or less a pseudo-Quaker who, like two of our presidents, found a faint aura of Quakerism profitable to a calculating, acquisitive career. But the Quakers represent something extremely important in the compound of American culture. They are probably the only group which enjoys universal prestige—except, of course, in Philadelphia. Insofar as America has a culture, it is a culture of mutual antagonisms. When the melting pot really melts, it produces only the anonymous, anomalous, homogenized, homogeneous, mass man. The pietistic traditions in America, which, one would presume, were committed to producing frictionless personalities who would adjust perfectly to communalist religious utopias, produced in fact quite the opposite. I think it is this tradition, rather than that of New England theocracy, which gave birth to populism, both literary and political, with all its many ramifications—the dream of free men in free communities making up a free society in a free nation. The initial impulse was Quaker and Pennsylvania Dutch, German Pietist, but it is the promise which their little societies first held forth that attracted the millions from northern Europe who filled up the Middle West, and from whom came the great progressive politicians who were defeated on April 17, 1917. These are the people who gave American socialism its special character—Eugene Debs came from the old French town of Terre Haute, just around the corner of the rivers from Robert Owen's New Harmony.

German influence remains strong in America from 1848 to the First War. St. Louis, Milwaukee, Cincinnati, Chicago, were amongst the most civilized provincial cities in the world, and their civilization was as international in its connections as that of New York, Boston, and Philadelphia.

After 1900 Jewish influence became increasingly strong and has endured, decreasing again, until the present time. From about 1910 to 1925 New York was one of the major capitals of Yiddish culture, a strong competitor with Warsaw or Frankfurt. Plays by the leading European playwrights were performed in the Yiddish Theater. A majority of the leading Yiddish writers came to America to visit, many of them to stay. Yiddish magazines and newspapers discussed the literature and drama, philosophy, and political theories of Europe for a general audience, when such issues were known only to a handful of intellectual English-speaking Americans. The influence was reciprocal. The American Populist writers were translated into Yiddish, or read in English by Yiddish writers. The poet Yehoash was a disciple of Ezra Pound. The influence of Yiddish writing itself on American literature in English was practically nil. In that direction the influence was largely personal or seminal and postponed for a generation, until the children of Yiddish speakers began to write in English. Then too the large number of Jews in the labor movement, especially in the garment trades, provided an audience for Socialist and syndicalist writers. They would cheer the anarchist poet Arturo Giovannitti when he recited his poems at mass meetings, even though they understood no Italian and little more English. Since this extraordinarily active Yiddish culture was isolated both by language and prejudice, it is without doubt the most underestimated factor in the American intellectual synthesis.

Chinese and Japanese literature did not enter the American mainstream from ethnic sources within the country until after the Second War, and then only slightly, in San Francisco, although imported Far Eastern culture played an important role as an outside influence on American poetry from 1890 on. Negro poetry and folksong is a separate and very important subject and will be treated later.

So much for culture in the sociological or anthropological sense. How does all this work out specifically in the evolution of American poetry? It would be a great mistake to think that an ethnic interpretation of literature would be exhaustively explanatory, any more than Hippolyte Taine's Hippocratic environmentalism of Earth, Air, and Water. It does, however, show why American literature should be far more open to international influences than that of more homogeneous countries like Sweden or Spain. But, it's not necessarily true. The children of immigrants notoriously renounce the ways of their parents.

When the twentieth century opened, American poetry had already acquired a substantial tradition, almost all of it accumulated in the later three quarters of the nineteenth century. These were the poets who were taught in school until well past the First World War: William Cullen Bryant, Ralph Waldo Emerson, Henry Wadsworth Longfellow, John Greenleaf Whittier, James Russell Lowell, and in the South, Sidney Lanier. The poets whom today we consider important were not taught in schools—Jones Very, Edward Taylor, Herman Melville, Emily Dickinson, were almost

14

completely unknown as poets. We have a very respectable tradition of Protestant spirituality in the American nineteenth century in these poets. All are concerned, like their Danish contemporary, Søren Kierkegaard, with the mystery of utter contingency over against absolute omnipotence, the existential dilemma—why being at all? Melville never became more than a great amateur poet, but Emily Dickinson is the equal of any woman poet of the century except Christina Rossetti and the Brontë sisters. Edgar Allan Poe and Walt Whitman were frowned on and only their most innocuous verse, "The Bells," "The Raven," and "O Captain, My Captain," were anthologized, or memorized by school children.

We think of Poe and Whitman as the only American poets of the nineteenth century with international reputations and influence, but this is an illusion of perspective. Most of the poets whose portraits once decorated the corridors of American grammar schools had very substantial European reputations. Baudelaire made more money from his translations of Poe than he did from anything else he wrote, but we forget, if we ever knew, that he was paid a substantial sum to translate "Hiawatha" (he never did it), and imitated "Hiawatha" in a poem of his own, "LE CALUMET DE PAIX"—IMITÉ DE LONGFELLOW; "*Or Gitche Manito, le Maître de la Vie.*"

Longfellow was probably the most internationally minded poet writing in his day and he poured into America translations, imitations and echoes of the literatures of all Europe. "Hiawatha" is an imitation of *The Kalevala* put together from folk songs and tales by the Finnish folklorist Lönnrött. Longfellow got his Indian mythology from Schoolcraft, but along with the trochaic meter of *The Kalevala* there is a subtle infusion of its strangely haunted stories. Longfellow was very much aware that he was attempting to supply the American people with mythological roots in their own land and for three generations he pretty much succeeded.

Emerson was seriously taken both in Great Britain and Germany, both as philosopher and poet, and he is still read in both countries, as the most successful popularizer of a kind of mean, or average, or common-denominator, late German Romantic philosophy of the more liberal persuasion, or perhaps as the forerunner of America's characteristic philosophy—individualist pragmatism. He also shared the interest of the international intellectual community of his time in the literature and philosophies of India and the Far East.

What distinguished America's major nineteenth-century writers was that, like the English, they were not alienated. They gave expression to the attitudes and opinions of most Americans. Even Whitman—even more than any of the others—for he was above all else the apostle of the American Dream, when that dream was still capable of passionate belief. There were *alienés* in America but they were peculiar people, separated from society by circumstance, like Emily Dickinson, or by a constitutional mental oddness, like Melville. Toward the end of his life Whitman probably came to realize that, at least within the context of post-Civil War American enterprise and Manifest Destiny, his dream had failed. Even so his alienation was largely posthumous.

Poe is a special case. "Jamais Plus" by Monsieur Poe is a classic of French literature. Poe's great reputation in France is due to the fact that his translators, Baudelaire and Mallarmé, were the greatest French poets of their times and more important, that they didn't understand English

16

all that well, even though Mallarmé taught it. What prestige Poe enjoys amongst modern American poets is due mostly to the reflection of his extraordinary French reputation and also somewhat to the propaganda of modern Southern writers—who even like Sidney Lanier. Tales of his genre are now considered quite respectable, the Gothic romance pushed to its extreme by the French and German Romantics. As a matter of fact, they are rather better than their European counterparts—with the exceptions of Kleist, Nerval, and E. T. A. Hoffman. Poe, too, perhaps more than any American writer, was a popularizer, and in spite of his Baudelairian life, anything but alienated. He is incidentally the only one of our leading writers of those times who was a professional—who tried to live by his pen.

In the early years of the twentieth century in the Protestant parts of the country that still clung to the old ways—Maine, Indiana, Kansas, Oregon—by far the most popular poet, and not just with school teachers, was Whittier. Now that two generations of literary contention have died away, it becomes possible to see that this judgment may almost have been right. Whittier in his narrow tradition is a very good poet indeed. In comparison with Longfellow his verse sounds like poetry, the work of a man who thought in aural-oral terms and not just in verbal. He is a better poet than Isaac Watts, the English hymn writer, or in fact than anyone else who wrote eighteenth-century Augustan quatrains, and he is better than all but a few who wrote narratives or reveries of nature. He was also, with the sole exception of Whitman, socially the most radical important American poet of the nineteenth century. Like Whitman, or like William Carlos Williams later, he was also supremely autochthonous, with a wonderful eye and ear for the sensory detail of the poetic situation—the especially American situation.

17

It is possible to trace parallels to Whittier in English and Continental verse of the seventeenth and eighteenth centuries, but parallels they remain. It is most unlikely that he ever heard of most of these writers.

Whittier was not only a popular poet, he was genuinely a poet of the people, and of that then still surviving majority of the American people whose revolution was still winning. It is practically impossible for a modern reader so to rearrange his mind that he can read "Hiawatha" or "Evangeline" or "Tales of a Wayside Inn" with pleasure, however often he may be moved to laughter. It requires little rearrangement and that only of superficial tastes for a socially responsible modern American to enjoy Whittier.

Whitman is the only American poet who from his day to ours has been a major world writer and who has influenced writers in every language—from Rabindranath Tagore, Francis Jammes, Emile Verhaeren, or Blaise Cendrars to the contemporary Matabele poet, Raymond Kunene. Whether we like it or not, and most Establishment critics do not, America has produced only one world writer, Walt Whitman. His only competitor is Mark Twain, but Mark Twain's one great book, *Huckleberry Finn,* has had little direct influence, while Whitman's influence has been decisive on writers in almost every known literature—Turkish, Japanese, Bengali, Hebrew, Urdu.

Whitman is special in another and most important way. Modern commercial, industrial Western civilization is the only one in history whose major artists have rejected all its values—Baudelaire, Blake, Hölderlin, down to T. S. Eliot, Voznesensky, or Allen Ginsberg. Every important poet since the rise of acquisitive, competitive, modern society has been alienated to a greater or lesser degree. Only two writers of the first rank successfully refused alienation and yet still speak meaningfully to us today—Tolstoy and Walt Whitman, the polar opposites of Baudelaire.

Critics of American society see it as the most extreme form of middle-class acquisitiveness. Whitman saw it as the very opposite, the promise of the ultimate fulfillment of all those virtues which today, to other peoples, it seems most to lack. In the latter part of the twentieth century terms like "The American Dream" and "The American Way of Life" sound like fraudulent propaganda or advertising slogans to us. They did not to Whitman. To him they were terms of a millenarian vision, an apocalypse in which every vestige of fraud or exploitation between human beings had been burned away.

Whitman grew up in, and was formed by, an environment in which such ideas were commonplace. We forget that America was founded by, and for fifty years or more ruled by, radical intellectuals. As they lost power in the years before the Civil War, their ideas went underground and surfaced in dozens of secular and religious communal sects, all seeking the community of love, the abode of peace, the cooperative commonwealth. Whitman's ideas were common currency in the radical Left of pre-Civil War America, all those to whom the Civil War would be an extension of the Revolutionary War and who would never realize they had lost it. Whitman's visionary democracy is quite unlike the rationalist, social-contract Utopia envisioned by the French Revolution. It is a community of love, of organic fulfillment in the comradeship of work, play, sex, the family, the family in which the self, far from being alienated, is liberated and universalized in joy with all the others. At every point Whitman offers an alternative to the ethics of the rising predatory society.

Whitman's poems are full of men doing things together.

In all his hymns to labor nobody seems to work for money, but for "nothing," for joy in work and in each other, a universal creativity in which each discovers his ultimate individuation. After work they loaf and admire the world, blow tunes on leaves of grass, or wander through calm First Day streets, arm in muscular arm, or make love in religious ecstasy. Most Utopias are really an idealized past moved into the future. Whitman's is a future which he thought of as perfectly practicable and almost certain to be realized, moved into the present. Faith, hope, and love: these are the virtues that make man human, and hope is joy in the presence of the future in the present. On hope all creativity depends. The creative act is work which brings past, present, and future together in enduring objects, experiences, relationships. In his great mystical poems Whitman says again and again that this is the principle of being itself. Being is realized in the community of work and love, and love and work, the meaning of the universe. Whitman is the poet of revolutionary hope, and without hope revolution is catastrophe.

But Whitman was more than a poet with a message. He is one of the great masters of Blake's minute particulars, more than an acute imagist, a poet whose images have not only perfect clarity, but profound significance. For Whitman the facts of life beneath his feet and before his eyes and in the grasp of his hands were the doors of vision.

In the years since *Leaves of Grass* was first published, scholars had sought everywhere for the sources of his verse. True, he was influenced by the Bible, especially by Isaiah—and by *Ossian,* Macpherson's pretended translations from the Gaelic. It is doubtful if he read any of Blake's prophetic books or was influenced by the free-verse experiments of Matthew Arnold.

20

There is nothing modern about free verse. It begins with Goethe's *Wanderers Sturmlied* in 1771, Macpherson's *Ossian*, Hölderlin, Blake and Novalis. Heine, Matthew Arnold and Nietzsche all wrote free verse before French *vers libre* was invented by Vielé-Griffin. It is unlikely that Whitman knew anything about, much less read, most of these poets— although Hölderlin's *Odes* (assumed to be like those of Pindar whose prosody was not understood in those days) and Novalis's *Hymns of Night,* which he wrote in strophic verse, but had printed as prose poetry, both bear an extraordinary resemblance to Whitman's most profound poems. They share with Whitman certain aspects of philosophy and language, especially in those poems that celebrate the mystery of death or that preach a social chiliasm.

Whitman's prosody is unique. There was nothing like it before, and it has never been successfully imitated since. His immediate disciples, Horace Traubel and Edward Carpenter, are, as poets, simply that, unsuccessful imitators. The free-verse poets directly in the Whitman tradition— Theodore Dreiser, Sherwood Anderson, Carl Sandburg, Arturo Giovannitti, Lola Ridge, James Oppenheim, Wallace Gould—were influenced by his example but do not directly echo his actual prosody. "Free verse" in fact is only incidental to the Whitman tradition. What is important is the development and transformation of his vision.

Whitman never lost his optimistic faith in the fulfillment of his American dream, but in the twentieth century it became increasingly apparent that that dream would never be realized in the society as then constituted. Anyone with a realistic estimate of the tendencies of that society would have known that *Leaves of Grass* demands a revolutionary change, but Whitman did not. It certainly became apparent from the Eighties on—with the abandonment of the objectives for which most men in the North thought they had fought the Civil War, and with the maturing of the Age of the Robber Barons in finance and industry, and the growth of an immense population of immigrant labor and Negroes who were shut out from the American way of life. Whitman's joyous workmen swinging their tools in the open air were replaced by a frustrated proletariat in the dark satanic mills, and his independent yeomen by heavily mortgaged farms, tenant farmers, farm laborers in that order of development. So the poetic followers of Whitman became, first, radical Populists like Vachel Lindsay, then Socialists like Carl Sandburg, then anarchists like Arturo Giovannitti, or Communists like Mike Gold. Between the wars it seemed as though the Whitman tradition was slowly dying, but it endured underground in hundreds of little magazines, and after the Second War emerged again in poets like Allen Ginsberg and then again swept the world.

II.

AFTER the mid-nineteenth century, in America as in England, people seemed to stop trying to be major poets. There is a long interim of very minor poets indeed, unrelieved by any American parallels to the English Decadents.

There were American Decadents—Edgar Saltus, George Sylvester Viereck, Sadakichi Hartmann—poets who thought of themselves as analogues of Oscar Wilde or Ernest Dowson, but they were not very good. Their audience was confined to bohemia. American poetry was dominated by popular versifiers like James Whitcomb Riley, Eugene Field, and Ella Wheeler Wilcox. Well-bred people read—in extremely small editions—genteel writers like George Santayana, Trumbull Stickney, Anna Hempstead Branch, Ridgely Torrence, Lizette Woodworth Reese, Louise Imogen Guiney, William Ellery Leonard, or the well-bred, facile, "vagabond" verse of Richard Hovey and the Canadian, Bliss Carman. Each of these people wrote at least one memorable poem, usually a sonnet, usually a revery. Anna Hempstead Branch stands out. Her "The Monk in the Kitchen" is a gently mystical poem, the imagined utterance of an ideal Brother Lawrence—and says, "Martha is equally the visionary with Mary." Her poetry is evidence that Emily Dickinson (who was practically unknown until long after her death) was not alone. Emily Dickinson, Jones Very,

23

Edward Taylor, and Anna Hempstead Branch together give a rare expression to the mysticism latent in the Puritan tradition. There are few Protestant mystics like them in any language.

Edward Markham, William Vaughn Moody, and Stephen Crane also stand out from the run-of-the-mill poets of the end of the century: Markham and Moody by their deeply felt social responsibility, and Crane by his anticipation of the twentieth century's "modern sensibility" and his free verse. Moody was probably, with the possible exception of the philosopher George Santayana, the most substantial mind among poets of his day. He died at forty while he was still growing as a poet and thinker. Stephen Crane was not a thinker at all. In fact what makes his little free-verse poems difficult to read today is their relentless pretensions to "philosophy." What is good about them is their occasional sharp sensate awareness.

In the whole period, from Walt Whitman and Emily Dickinson to Edwin Arlington Robinson and Robert Frost, the greatest American poet is Stuart Merrill, and second to him, Vielé-Griffin. Both lived abroad and wrote in French.

"The genteel tradition," the Harvard Wits, and the American imitators of the literary establishment of late Victorian England, developed a style that was to endure for a long time, so that even today, even fairly sophisticated critics think of it as the normal way to write. Edmund Wilson has written a few nostalgic, tragic, love reveries in this style that are far too little known. The style was too diffused to be called that of a school, and the best of its writers differed from the early Georgian poets in England in the traces they showed of the influence of the more sentimental French Symbolists and the English Decadents, especially Ernest Dowson and Richard Le Gallienne. Those poets who read the popular French poetry of their time give evidence of having also enjoyed the work of the *Fantaisistes,* Tristram Derême, P.-J. Toulet and their friends, who published in the *Mercure de France* and *Le Divan.* The resemblance of the best of Arthur Davidson Ficke to Derême can hardly be accidental. In a sense these sonneteers of sentimental revery, erotic nostalgia and *Schwärmerei* would find a later spokesman in Conrad Aiken. Today we forget that this was once an international idiom, as widespread as its contemporary *Art nouveau* and *Jugendstil* in the plastic arts. Carefully translated into French or German, the verse of Witter Bynner, Arthur Davidson Ficke, Louis Untermeyer, Jean Starr Untermeyer, Orrick Johns, would seem quite at home. The style would last well past the mid-century with such poets as John Hall Wheelock, Louis Untermeyer, and Robert Hillyer and a host of lesser writers. Curiously, it was this style which dominated the poetry of the magazines of the political Left, *Mother Earth,* the old *Masses, The Liberator.* Even the Yiddish Socialist and anarchist papers published such poetry almost exclusively. Max Eastman, the dominant editor of *Masses* and *The Liberator,* thought of himself above all else as a great lover and romantic bard and wrote poetry to fit the role. He died happy as an editor of *Reader's Digest.* His politics changed, but not his taste. Well before the First World War it was already established that revolutionary esthetics meant simply lower middle-class sentimentality. The entire Populist-Socialist-anarchist style which developed from Whitman had to fight its way against greater opposition from the taste of Left politicians and bureaucrats than ever it met from bourgeois editors. This of course is still true, all over the world.

I hope I will not be accused of being an anti-feminist—but we have to face the fact that America in the nineteenth and early twentieth century was the home, above all else, and above all other countries, of lady poetry—sentimental, melodramatic, verging on artificial hysteria, overwritten and carelessly written, sometimes rather sweetly modest, but most often pretentious. The outstanding post-War I spokesman, or spokeslady, for this sort of thing was Edna St. Vincent Millay, the successor to Ella Wheeler Wilcox, her like number of the 1900's. One of the leading anthologists of the period slyly groups her in a chapter with her various lovers. The best poetry by women in fact was written by feminists, revolutionaries, or lesbians. The sexual revolution was certainly necessary and it was passionately fought by women who dedicated the whole of themselves, but it produced verse that seldom rose above bad imitation of Elizabeth Barrett Browning—who was hardly a suffragette. Liberated they were, but from what? From restraint. Not just the sexual restraint of the public morality of the era, but from artistic restraint. The most devastating criticism of the whole school is the analysis of a sonnet of Edna St. Vincent Millay's by I. A. Richard's students (who had no idea who she was) in his book, *Practical Criticism,* or the similar analysis of "Euclid Alone Has Looked on Beauty Bare," her most famous sonnet, in *Directions in Modern Poetry* by Elizabeth Drew and John L. Sweeney.

Sara Teasdale, Helen Hoyt, Marjorie Allen Seiffert, Margaret Widdemer, Rose O'Neil, Hazel Hall, Genevieve Taggard, Jean Starr Untermeyer, and hundreds of lesser ladies dominate the little magazines and the "class" magazines like *Century, Scribner's, Harper's,* and *The Atlantic* (where they still survive) of the time. Apparently the best way to get a poem published in a "class" magazine in America is to start off with the line, "Beloved, the stars reach down

26

and strangle me"—even today. Perhaps half the population who reads at all believes that that is what poetry is. Strangely, most of the verse of Amy Lowell, a lady for whom the word "redoubtable" was invented, belongs, for all her passionate championing of "the modern movement," in this category. Yet she was born emancipated and seems to have had scarcely any erotic life at all. However synthetic the poetry of most of these women seems, most of them actually lived it, or, in contemporary psychiatric slang, "acted it out." It is sad reading them over today. I knew most of them, at least slightly, and most of them lived tragic lives indeed, and a very large proportion were suicides.

By contrast the women poets who have survived in contemporary taste as specially feminine were precisely that, subtle analysts of feminine sensitivity, psychology, and the disabilities of women in the erotic relationship. Eunice Tietjens, Elinor Wylie, Elizabeth Coatsworth, Louise Bogan, Evelyn Scott, Leonie Adams, Elizabeth Madox Roberts, Marya Zaturenskaya, are distinguished from the women I have mentioned in the preceding paragraph by their control and their understanding. Looking at them as a group they seem to embody a type that has vanished from the earth, the cultivated intellectual woman of the first third of the century. They are a group of Henry James heroines. After all, why not? The ideal Edwardian woman quite possibly was exactly what her society called her, "the finest product of Western Civilization."

Babette Deutsch, who is usually grouped with the others, is something else, as Horace Gregory once said of her, "a true gentlewoman of letters," naturally emancipated and at ease in literature. Like Eunice Tietjens, Babette Deutsch does not try to use literature. Her values are those of action and the experience that results from that action, rather than a description of secondary or tertiary qualities of things in hierarchies.

From 1890 on there was a whole world of poets who were influenced by the French Symbolists and the English Decadents. They still exist. They are the bohemian underworld of Greenwich Village bars, and cafés, and little magazines, and candlelit studio parties. At the beginning of the century the most outstanding personality was Sadakichi Hartmann. Half German, half Japanese, he came to America in late adolescence and almost immediately was writing poems, translating from French and German, giving lectures on the European avant-garde of the day, and generally playing the role of an Atlantic bridge. He visited Mallarmé and talked to him about Whitman. He visited Whitman and talked to him about Mallarmé. He wrote plays in imitation of Strindberg's Symbolist dramas, and poems in imitation of Verlaine and his *poètes maudits,* of Charles Cros and Carco. There was only one thing wrong with his poems: they were simply awful. Yet he knew more than anybody else and he seemed to know everybody. One of the great talkers of all time, he held self-taught intellectuals from the Middle West and students from Harvard spellbound in the Liberal Club, Polly Holliday's, The Dutch Oven, Grace's Garrett, and The Purple Pup in the years just before, during, and just after the First War, as he had entranced Huneker, Robert W. Chambers, Ludwig Lore, Ben de Casseres, and Vance Thompson in Lüchow's when the century was new.

This old-time bohemia was peculiarly German in its mentors, its connections, and its style, both of literature and life. The plays and poems of Sadakichi Hartmann, Edgar Saltus, George Sylvester Viereck, and their friends were really bad German Expressionism, rather than French Symbolism, and they can be read only with embarrassed hilarity today. Yet these people were more right than their respectable contemporaries. From *Mlle New York* to Joe Kling's *Pagan* their literary, social, and political opinions were forty years in advance of the great movement of alienation and revolt that swept the country after 1950. Their influence on the classic American modernists, when the latter were young, was profound, although only Ezra Pound has ever talked about it. He has said that if he hadn't been himself, the next best thing would be to have been Sadakichi.

It is so easy for literary historians to overlook literary bohemia, but from the beginning it has always been there, a background from which more accomplished writers and more respectable writing emerged, and which provided them with the essential interconnection of a social environment. Much of the work of Conrad Aiken and Mina Loy, and the early poems of Eliot and Pound, are only better, more etherialized, versions of the poetry current in the bohemias of their youth; and a poet like Maxwell Bodenheim was a pure bohemian who almost managed to be accepted, and to this day he is found in most anthologies.

The impact of purely personal influence is hard to measure, but it can be decisive. To take an imaginary case, we could think of Sadakichi saying to Carl Sandburg, "When you get to Belgium be sure and look up Verhaeren. He's a friend of mine and speaks English," or reading aloud Alfred Jarry's *Ubu Roi* or the poems of Tristan Corbière to an audience of Harvard boys that included T. S. Eliot (I am not sure that these two cases *are* imaginary).

Then too, the politics of the bohemians of the first twenty years of the century was very important, forgotten for years and resurrected in our own time. They were mostly anarchists, a mixture of Kropotkin, Alexander Berkman, and Emma Goldman, who were of course part of their circle, of Nietzsche, Max Stirner, and half-understood Oriental mysticism. It was through Sadakichi Hartmann and another bohemian, Lafcadio Hearn, and Yone Noguchi, the father of Isamu, that American writers first learned about the poetry of Japan and China.

What used to be called the modern movement in poetry is usually considered to have begun with the early work, in each case their second books, of Edwin Arlington Robinson and Robert Frost. Rather the opposite is true. Both Robinson and Frost revived the main tradition of nineteenth-century American poetry, of Bryant, Longfellow, Whittier, Lowell. True, they do not resemble any of these poets enough to be called disciples, but neither do they resemble one another, nor did the major American poets of the nineteenth century.

It is also true that Robinson's bitter irony and Frost's Yankee-hermit *persona* reveal a degree of alienation unknown to their predecessors. Frost has been called "Whittier without the whiskers," but Whittier thought of himself as speaking to, and from, and within the American public, whereas Frost's first-person character speaks from outside, from a New England hill farm bypassed by industrial, competitive, urban civilization. Whittier in fact was a good deal odder personally than Robert Frost, but in his day no one ever thought of him as a "character," while Frost's personality and his poetry were formed by role-playing. Both Robinson and Frost were also much more dependent upon English ancestors than were the men of the nineteenth century. Both were strongly influenced by Crabbe, Tennyson's narrative poems, and by Browning and Hardy. Both also were closely related to early twentieth-century English poets—the Georgian school. Robert Frost discovered his own special medium while living in rural England near the rural poet Edward Thomas. Robinson's famous irony is paralleled amongst the Georgians by the less facile but more profound dramatic poems of Harold Munro. Both Frost and Robinson have been without significant disciples. They were the end, not the beginning of a tradition.

There is a large body of amateur poetry, from the poetry columns of New England newspapers to the work of Senator Eugene McCarthy, which might be called the school of Robert Frost. Much of it is very good indeed, in a quiet way, but it enjoys no intellectual prestige, and it is not published in the literary quarterlies. Both men, but Frost especially, have been inflated into public myths by the more conservative critics. It is interesting to sit down for an evening and read alternately poems by Edward Thomas and Robert Frost or Robinson and Harold Munro. It gives one a sense of critical scale. The Englishmen, who are certainly not "major poets," are in many ways the better writers. A comparison with the "dramatic lyrics" of Thomas Hardy is even more revealing.

Robinson and Frost have often been called Realist writers and, compared with the European Realist novel which presumably begins with Balzac, Stendhal, and Constant, are considered as part of an American movement from Realism to Naturalism which includes William Dean Howells, Harold Frederic, David Graham Philips, Frank Norris, Theodore Dreiser. Strictly speaking, America never had any significant Realist novelists of major importance, although around the turn of the century what was then called "local color fiction," especially of the South, was extremely popular. Neither were there many Naturalist writers, American disciples of Zola. The reason is simple. Most American fiction to this day is more tendentious than European. Dreiser, Frank Norris, even a local color writer like Kate Chopin, the author of a passionately feminist novel, are far more tendentious than even Zola in *Nana* and *Germinal,* much less Maupassant, whom they all admired greatly. American fiction almost always has a moral at the end, unwritten but as obvious as any copybook story, and only at the best more cleverly concealed than in the novels of Upton Sinclair. Edgar Lee Masters' *Spoon River Anthology* (is it a Realist, Naturalist, or Populist work?) was a more important turning point than anything by Frost or Robinson. Read with attention the little epitaphs make up a grim novel, a Balzacian *comédie humaine* of a small prairie town. In addition, the poem to his mother, "Lucinda Matlock," is one of the finest of the period. Alas, Masters never rose to such heights again.

The super-Realist tradition of Stendhal and Flaubert passes to Henry James and is reflected in the poetry of Pound, Eliot, and Aiken. The poems of Robinson and Frost resemble more. than anything else the novels of Thomas Hardy, who I suppose could be called a Flaubertian without Flaubert's obsession with perfect style, the *mot juste,* but with *le mot brut.*

The best term for the American "realists" is probably Populist, and as years went on, if only the word had not become a shibboleth, Social, or even Socialist, Realist. Norris, Jack London, Upton Sinclair are all immensely popular in Russia. Interestingly there are, when you come to think of it, no Russian novelists of the same period to compare with them—except Gorky.

If the modern movement in poetry has a definite beginning it is either the publication of Carl Sandburg's *Chicago*

Poems or the first Imagist anthology, *Des Imagistes.* For the first works of Ezra Pound and William Carlos Williams were anything but "modernistic," that *A Lume Spento* of Pound's and William Carlos Williams' *The Tempers* are if anything deliberately anachronistic and Pound's verse remains a derivitive mixture of Pre-Raphaelitism, the English Decadence, Verlaine, and Remy de Gourmont until, precisely, the inauguration of the Imagist movement.

Harriet Monroe and her Chicago magazine, *Poetry,* have been given almost sole credit for the launching of modern American verse. *Reedy's Mirror,* edited by William Marion Reedy in St. Louis, played, in the early days, almost as important a role, and published first several of the people later claimed as discoveries by Miss Monroe, and there were other magazines of a more fugitive character, especially in the Middle West, but in New York, New Orleans, and San Francisco as well.

Between 1900 and the First War a movement of transformation and revaluation in the arts swept the world. The process had begun earlier in France. After Cezanne, Seurat, Mallarmé, and Rimbaud, French painting and poetry would never be the same again. After 1880 it became impossible to write like Lamartine or Hugo or paint like Delacroix or even Courbet. French Cubists, Italian Futurists, Russian Futurists, and Rayonnists were the contemporaries of Carl Sandburg and the Imagists. Compared to what was happening in other countries (except England), the American break was slight and occurred late.

A generation ago René Taupin created a minor critical sensation with his *L'Influence du symbolisme français sur la poésie américaine* (1929). He makes quite a bit of the influence of the Symbolists on the Imagists. His opinions have been repeated often since, but he is misleading. Imagism was a perfectly natural development in the main tradition of poetry in the English languages.

The Imagist Manifesto and Pound's "Don'ts for Imagists" say very little that wasn't said a century before by Wordsworth and Coleridge in the Preface to *Lyrical Ballads*. Poetry in English goes through cycles and swings every couple of generations from rhetoric to objectivity and back again. Amy Lowell's *Six French Poets* and Ezra Pound's long essay on modern French poetry are a sufficient indication of the knowledge of the leading Imagists of French poetry. There was one exception; the young English poet F. S. Flint, who was more knowledgable of his French contemporaries than almost anybody before or since, and who remains one of the best translators of the classic French modernists.

There was one direct personal influence. The Belgian (Walloon) poet, Jean de Bosschère, lived in London in those years, making a poor living as a French tutor. He was a close friend of Flint (who translated his *The Closed Door* —*La Porte fermée*). Published in England and America *face en face* with beautiful calligraphic illustrations by Bosschère, the poems were unlike anything that had ever been seen in English and had a tremendous influence on the Imagists, on Pound and Eliot who also knew Bosschère well, and most notably on James Joyce who has told people that Bosschère's poem, "Ulysse batie son lit" (Ulysses builds his bed), was an influence or at least inspiration for Joyce's *Ulysses*. This is a very good example of what cross-cultural influences are really like. A writer or artist or musician, without great reputation in his own country, may in translation have a significant effect in another culture, just as Samuel Smiles' *Self-Help in Chinese* was very popular

34

with the Confucian revivalists of the early years of the first Chinese Revolution.

At their first appearance the Imagists looked like much more of a coherent school than they really were, for the simple reason that they all appeared equally odd to the general public. Pound in those days was the last of the Pre-Raphaelites, and much given to what Dudley Fitts once called "Ye olde tea shoppe English." Richard Aldington was a sentimental erotic poet of the type of Pierre Loüys—with whom he shared a deliberate, self-conscious exoticism. John Gould Fletcher was the only one of the group actually much influenced by French Symbolism. But it was a neo-Symbolism of a kind represented by Remy de Gourmont and interpreted for English speakers by Arthur Symons—in other words as adjusted to the English Decadents. His color symphonies may owe something to René Ghil, as well as to Gourmont. The two poets who most literally exemplified the commandments of the Imagist Manifesto were F. S. Flint and Amy Lowell. The only trouble was they weren't very good poets. F. S. Flint had great charm and his simple personal poems carry the conviction of intimate confession. Amy Lowell managed to demonstrate in her poetry the paradox that the language of verse could be in contemporary speech; its images could be sharp and apposite with a high degree of sensory awareness, natural knowledge, and psychological insight; it could carefully eschew rhetorical devices; and yet be verbose and boring. Reading her poems one's mind is constantly blue penciling her precious images—as redundant as any rhetoric—and it is only in translations from the Chinese, done with Florence Ayscough, *Fir Flower Tablets,* and in some of her close imitations of the Chinese in *Pictures of the Floating World* that she is readable today at all. Even the Chinese translations are unduly wordy because she and Florence Ayscough, like Ezra Pound, believed in expanding the implicit meaning of the components of every Chinese ideogram. This was an indoor sport or parlor game amongst the Chinese literati of the last dynasty and misled many a Western translator.

H. D. (Hilda Doolittle who married Richard Aldington in the days when Imagism was in flower, with Pound playing Cupid and Best Man) has often been called the one perfect Imagist. That she was, but she was something more. In the first place she was a woman of the most extraordinarily delicate and grave beauty and her poetry is the poetry of a woman who knows she is very beautiful. When they were all together and young in London she was probably the best read of the Imagists, and the most open to poetry in other languages. In a sense she was the most international of them, but it was not the internationalism of the new classicism, whose most sensational representatives were the Cubist painters, but the internationalism of the Doric and Sapphic sensibility whose representatives were Renée Vivien in France, Walter Pater, and the two women who called themselves Michael Field in England, and Stefan George in Germany, and whose most popular single book was Pierre Loüys' *Les Chansons de Bilitis.* Her husband, Richard Aldington, wrote for her a little book of deliberate imitations of *Les Chansons de Bilitis, Myrrhina and Konalis,* which shares with Pierre Loüys and Swinburne the peculiar hysterical sentimentality of men imagining themselves women.

So too, H.D.'s Greece was a land that never was, the ideal Greece of Henri de Regnier, Paul Valéry, Swinburne's *Atalanta in Calydon,* and most especially, of Walter Pater. This is a Greece which enters modern culture through the

German critic Winckelmann and his practical disciple, the sculptor Thorvaldson, a Greece impossibly purified, in which people become crystalline symbols, a kind of animated Platonic Ideas. This is a Greece which most people believe once really existed, but whose existence in the public imagination is largely due to the fact that the garish paint and gilt has washed off the white marble statuary. A great deal of H.D. is slowed down, heavily weighted, more genuinely sensory *Atalanta in Calydon*. Her metric is something else—like Whitman's, a unique, purely personal discovery. There is nothing in European literature at all like it. Her sources are Sappho, the choruses of Euripides with his hypnotic rhythms of hyperaesthesia slipping into vertigo and then into trance. No one before or since had ever more perfectly mastered strophic verse. It is interesting to compare hers with the neo-classic poems of Paul Valéry. H.D.'s are stripped to the absolute essentials. The sensibility has worn away all extraneous matter as time has worn away the Parthenon, while Valéry's purist poems are cluttered with the residues of his century's studio conversations.

There are other people in the Imagist anthologies who didn't belong there—D. H. Lawrence, the forgotten poet, Skipwith Cannell, and, of all people, James Joyce.

As is well known, once she heard of the Imagists, Amy Lowell came to London as soon as she conveniently could and took over the movement, with all the aggressive manipulative techniques of a musical-comedy impresario, or a modern public relations firm. Pound withdrew immediately and after a couple of years the others, tired of being pushed around, went their separate ways. If Amy Lowell did nothing else she got poetry into the newspapers, but she also identified modern poetry in the public mind with little movements, cliques, and manifestoes. All this resulted in substantial sales for herself, but interestingly, it did not do so for the others. It took years for H.D.'s books to sell more than a few hundred copies, and even more years for Pound to become genuinely popular, even amongst the highly literate.

III.

To paraphrase the Communist Manifesto, a spectre has haunted American poetry for over half a century, the obstreperous presence of Ezra Pound. He has educated, propagandized, promoted, and demoted two generations of poets. Yet, as Gertrude Stein said of him, "He is a village explainer, excellent if you are a village, but if not, not." He has the reputation of having been a tireless discoverer and encourager of new talent, but as a matter of fact he tired rather early. After the invention and organization of the Imagist movement and then the championing of T. S. Eliot, Wyndham Lewis, Gaudier-Brzeka, and James Joyce and his propagandizing for Wyndham Lewis' Vorticist movement, a British would-be competitor with Cubism and Futurism (which Pound didn't understand), he lost his grip on the latest thing. Something in his private life happened in England that drove him to the continent and he lost touch with the developments in British and American poetry. Still, in his magazine *Exiles* in the mid-Twenties he managed to "discover" Louis Zukofsky, Carl Rakosi, Kenneth Fearing, Herman Spector, no mean accomplishment for one so far away, in every sense, from the American scene. However, he was of the opinion that his greatest discovery was a mediocre imitator of Swinburne and Ernest Dowson, one

Ralph Cheever Dunning, whom many people thought he had invented as a hoax.

The strongest, most direct personal influence on Ezra Pound is usually said to be T. E. Hulme, a strange bully-boy disciple of Georges Sorel and Bergson, whose five little *japoneries* appended to Pound's *Lustra* as "The Complete Poetical Works of T. E. Hulme" are considered the first Imagist poems. Hulme died in the war, but his influence on Pound endured. It was Hulme's Bergsonism and Bergsonism's literary reflection in the now-forgotten movement *unanimism* of Jules Romains that certainly was one of the sources of the method of the *Cantos*. No one reads Romains' poetry any more, and his immense series of novels, *Men of Good Will,* is read only for the historical perspectives on the first half of the twentieth century in a very soft mind. The most important *unanimiste* novel is John Dos Passos' *U.S.A.* If there is any satisfaction in labels, the *Cantos* could certainly be called the most important *unanimiste* poem.

Pound's career is divided sharply into three periods. The Pre-Raphaelite and the Decadent poetry of his first, almost ten, years in England, *A Lume Spento, Provenza, Personae,* then the poems of *Ripostes, Lustra, Cathay,* and *Poems 1918–21,* and last the exclusive concentration on the *Cantos.* Certainly the middle period is as a whole the best. This was the time of the great Chinese translations and the Noh plays (both from the manuscripts of Ernest Fenellosa), of great short poems like "Δωρια," "The Return," and "The Villanelle of the Psychological Hour," "Hugh Selwyn Mauberley," the paraphrases of Sextus Propertius and the first ten "cantos." Pound was not only at his peak as a poet in those days; he was teaching Yeats how to write Noh plays and teaching his dancers how to dance them before the amazed Micho Ito came along and took over. Not only Yeats, whose *Plays for Dancers* are certainly amongst his best drama, but also Sturge Moore whose Noh plays, though rather chilly and a little too obviously designed for the drawing rooms of Duchesses, as for that matter were Yeats', are likewise amongst his very best work.

Pound was the foreign editor of *Poetry Magazine* and after that of *The Little Review,* writing violent letters, attempting to civilize and Europeanize Miss Monroe, who obstinately remained devoted to the dynamos in the Chicago Water Tower, the steel mills of Gary, and the green cornfields all about. He was more successful with Margaret Anderson, who moved *The Little Review* to New York, and then to Paris, and who with her co-editor Jane Heap, and her schoolmaster, Ezra Pound, turned it into the first genuinely international magazine of the contemporary arts in the English language.

Pound explained Henry James to the audiences of Theodore Dreiser and David Graham Phillips. He explained modern French poetry, not very well, to the up and coming poets in the American colleges. He invented a new list of the "Hundred Best Books" sort, more germane to the modern mind than The Harvard Classics, The Five Foot Shelf, more germane for that matter than the much later list of Messers Mortimer Adler and Robert Hutchins (or was it Scott Buchanan?). For almost ten years, ending with 1921, Pound did not, in Pater's words, "Burn with a hard, gem-like flame"; he blazed like a forest fire. It is in those years that he helped to give shape and direction to all poetry in the English language since.

Pound may have been an excellent village explainer but America in the second and third decade of the twentieth century was intellectually a village. It is not that there were not plenty of people about with good taste, learning, and familiarity with European culture, and with complex sensibilities. There were. That's what the novels of Henry James were about; and, contrary to latter-day opinion, his novels made him a good living; but it is the very point of those novels that the old American elite had become creatively impotent and closed away in their own little garrison society, the genuine high society that never got into the society columns of the newspapers.

The intellectual, cultural, the very moral synthesis, of the earlier America had ceased to have vital meaning for its descendants. (The best examples are Francis Brooks and Henry Adams.) It had become indeed the "genteel tradition." Meanwhile there had grown up around gentility a new barbarism anxious to find its own elite. They were not only the majority of the literate; they were by far the most creative, and they certainly were hungry, for culture, for status, and simply for information.

The old elite had lived in a kind of Girondin-physiocrat utopia constructed in their own imaginations, while the imperialist, industrial, competitive America of the Robber Barons and the Spanish American War, the Philippine War, and the destruction of Reconstruction had made their dream community meaningless. It had not made Whitman's new order of the ages meaningless; quite the contrary; it had made it an enemy; but there were hundreds of young writers who could not assimilate or be assimilated by the Populist-turned-revolutionary tradition. And for them Pound was teacher and organizer. He was perfectly well aware of his role and was fond of comparing himself to Lenin, writing angry letters from abroad to the provincially minded Bolshevik home guard. He deliberately set out to teach the simplest elements, the basic foundations of culture, how to read and how to write. "Too many adjectives!" "Throw out the inversions!" "Fact, not rhetoric!" "Don't tell them how you feel, make them feel it!" "Don't imitate your contemporaries!" "Read the classics, especially in foreign languages! You can't imitate *them!*" It all reads as if it were written in blue pencil in the margins of sophomore papers. At no point was there anything wrong with Pound's advice, but he was speaking to a classroom where nobody had ever read the hundred best books, and whose ideas of how to write had been shaped by the commercial magazines, or even worse, by the genteelly dishonest "class" magazines, of which there were far more in those days than there are now.

Scarcely anyone who first read "Homage to Sextus Propertius" had ever heard of Propertius and even the reviewers in the highbrow magazines referred to him as "an obscure Latin poet." What did it matter that Pound's quantitative free verse was a softer, dreamier echo of the hard, elegiac distiches of Propertius? Pound's verse was better than anybody else's at that moment and opened up new prosodic regions for poets who would come after him.

Pound's Chinese translations and his Noh plays made Far Eastern literature meaningful in the context of modern society. There had been translations of Oriental literature before. Yone Noguchi, E. Powys Mathers, and Lafcadio Hearn had made a sentimental *Art nouveau japonerie* popular amongst the teacups of the culture klatches of the American hinterland, and other even less skilled writers had translated Oriental poetry into sterile doggerel. Stuart Merrill translated an anthology of French prose poetry, *Pastels in Prose,* which included beautiful poems from Judith Gautier's *Livre du jade.* Judith Gautier was a far greater poet than Noguchi or Hearn, but she too suffers the com-

43

mon fault of the older Oriental translators. They all expand the meanings, and bring out the implicits, which they think they find in the verse, and what they find is usually sentimental, and even if not, always softens the impact. Pound created a style that the Western world will think of as specifically that of Far Eastern poetry for a long, long time to come. A few years later he would be followed in America by Amy Lowell and Florence Ayscough with their more diffuse *Fir Flower Tablets* and by Witter Bynner's altogether excellent *The Jade Mountain*. In England, contemporary with Pound, Arthur Waley was more accurately translating Chinese and Japanese poetry, and later also prose into excellent but less thrilling language. Pound's "The River Merchant's Wife" is one of the greatest poems in American literature, a free translation of Li Po.

In the poems of the *Ripostes, Lustra, Cathay* period Pound established, to use Whitehead's term, the mode of presentational immediacy as the method with which the poetic sensibility could cope with the modern world. He has probably had a wider influence by now on writers all over the world than even Apollinaire, who is usually thought of as the human watershed of modern poetry. Much of this influence is of a latter growth than the immediate post-War One period, and stems from the *Cantos*. Pound's most important disciple in those years was T. S. Eliot, who was to dominate the interbellum period.

So back to the other tradition. The writers who learned from Pound were, most of them, what later would be called elitist. But the function of an elite is to lead a society. They seceded from the mass culture, from middle-class values, from commercialism, and prided themselves on the smallness of their audience.

The Populists, on the other hand, met the predatory

society head on and challenged it at every point. They were not only Socialists and single-taxers, and apostles of Edward Bellamy's *Looking Backward,* and anarchists and utopians and communalists; as writers they and their allies in the academy all shared a specifically American philosophy of the social responsibility of the intelligentsia, a mystical projection of Vernon Parrington, Thorstein Veblen, John Dewey. Behind Harriet Monroe's Chicago Renaissance lay a mystique of Middle America, an inheritance not just from Whitman but from the reformers, communalists, and radical Abolitionists of the years before the Civil War. Sandburg's poem to the beautiful suffragette Inez Mulholland might just as well have been written to Victoria Claffin. Louis Sullivan, Frank Lloyd Wright, Vachel Lindsay, dozens of others—from the Spanish American War to the First World War—developed a whole ideology, a theory of a kind of homey America, a culture of country grocery stores, general farms with small but stately homes and statelier barns, small shops, skilled mechanics, bosky suburbs with overarching maples and elms, with porch swings, paper routes and Airedales for the young, the utopia of the Oz books, the ecology of Ernest Thompson Seton. It was an ideology which was no sooner formulated than it was seen to be irrelevant. Anything like it could never be achieved by reform and was unlikely to come about by revolution, but for thirty years it had almost existed.

One by one its political spokesmen were defeated or coöpted by the Establishment. Thomas Reed, that wanderer from the Senate of the Roman Republic, could not stop the Philippine War. Bryan, LaFollette, Norris, Wheeler, Rankin, Hiram Johnson could not prevent Wilson's War. Massive strikes, bitterly fought class war convulsed towns like the one where Thoreau's family once had a pencil factory. The old elite became jingoists like Theodore Roosevelt, and after the war a committee of Brahmins, the purest products of New England, would electrocute Sacco and Vanzetti. Implicit in Whitman's "To a Foiled European Revolutionaire," and his other poems on the Paris Commune and similar struggles abroad, is the notion that here in America all that is behind us; and ahead of us lies only the positive task of building the community of love. Such dreams were due for a rude awakening. While the century was still young, the old optimistic voices gave way to voices in prison—Emma Goldman, Alexander Berkman, Arturo Giovannitti, Big Bill Haywood and his IWW soapboxers and Eugene Victor Debs, the perfect symbol and spokesman of the dream of Middle America.

The dream was extraordinarily perdurable in literature. Vachel Lindsay never lost it, but it became the dream of a broken heart. Edgar Lee Masters knew it was false, but never found anything to put in its place. The group around James Oppenheim's *Seven Arts,* which overlapped Alfred Stieglitz's circle of photographers, painters, and poets around *261* and *Camera Work,* still believed faithfully, even after the First War; but their brightest, noblest spokesman, Randolph Bourne, broke away and moved far to the Left. Their principal recruit from the new generation, Hart Crane, tried once again to write the epic of the American Dream. As one goes down the list of the poets of this faith one soon discovers that the majority of them committed suicide.

Sandburg did not commit suicide. He started out a typical young man in a Middle Western small town before the turn of the century, worked at odd jobs, went briefly to the Spanish American War on the relatively quiet front of Puerto Rico, came home, went to little Midwestern Lombard College in Galesburg, Illinois, his birthplace.

Again he worked at odd jobs, white-collar jobs this time, and then became a full-time organizer and speaker for the Social Democratic Party. He continued working for the Socialist movement after he became a newspaper reporter and he continued to work as a reporter and later a movie critic in Chicago long after he became famous. (Actually his job as movie critic for the *Chicago Daily News* was finally a sinecure. His name appeared as a byline but the copy was written by ghosts. It was the publisher's method of patronage, profitable to both sides. The only trouble was, most people in Chicago thought it must be some other Carl Sandburg.) In 1903 he published a little pamphlet of poems of agricultural and industrial America. They seem naïve and amateurish today, but they compared more than favorably with the poems in the Socialist newspapers of the time. In 1914 Harriet Monroe published him in *Poetry, A Magazine of Verse* and he found himself famous. His poem "Chicago" became and remained the city's national anthem. At two-year intervals from then on he published *Chicago Poems, Corn Huskers, Smoke and Steel, Slabs of the Sunburnt West,* and in 1927 *The American Song Bag,* the first comprehensive collection of American folk song of all sorts, and still one of the best. After that, in *Good Morning, America, The People, Yes,* the biography of Abraham Lincoln, and the three collections of children's stories, his work steadily declined.

What happened to Sandburg? In the first place, he never recovered from the police reporter's hardboiled sentimentality that mars the work of all the Chicago school who worked for newspapers in his time, from Ben Hecht to the immensely learned and exquisitely esthetic Samuel Putnam. Many of the poems of his three first, best, books are highly compressed little human interest stories not unlike Ben

Hecht's *Thousand and One Afternoons in Chicago,* which ran as a *daily* column in the *Chicago Daily News.* Hecht's self-consciously pointed anecdotes are, to speak paradoxically, superficially more profound. What distinguishes Sandburg's "Dynamiter" and "Anna Imroth" is identification. He speaks for and from his own kind. It is the difference between empathy, properly used, and sympathy, the word it has incorrectly replaced in current jargon. What Sandburg had for the poor, frustrated, heroic, and ordinary, was *Einfühlung.*

What he also had was a marvelous prosody, a perfect ear for the beautiful potentials of common speech, something he learned from folk song, but mostly he learned from just listening—on a hundred jobs, at ball games, fishing for catfish, soldiering in Puerto Rico, swapping lies in the City Room or in the nearby bar, talking to militant "hunkies, kikes, and dagoes" after a Socialist speech. Listen to him on one of the old records reading the early poems, or singing, "I know moonlight, I know starlight, I lay this body down." There's never been anything like it, nor will there be again. That America is gone forever, with its folk culture, its folk ways, its folk song, its folk speech, and has been replaced by the mass culture, one part of which of course is the synthetic folk song revival of the Youth Revolt. It all came so naturally to him. When Sandburg tried to do the same thing deliberately, to construct two book-length epics of the vanishing folk life of the American common people, it didn't come off. *Good Morning, America* and *The People, Yes* are self-conscious and cooked. But by that time Sandburg had become a platform personality, singing for high-school assemblies the bitter ballad "Samuel Hall" with an expurgated chorus—"Gol durn your hides" instead of "I hates you one and all, damn your eyes."

Everybody loved Carl Sandburg in our town. Nobody knows where he went. I know where he went. In the last, latter years of the First War he was stationed in Stockholm as a foreign correspondent, able in that neutral capital, where he more or less spoke the language, to keep track of rumors, plots, peace feelers, and the lies of spies and counter-spies. He had become a militant Left-wing Socialist, a follower of Debs and Haywood, and his poems had been fearlessly anti-war. After the February Revolution in Russia, his relations with the Bolsheviks across the Baltic Sea become mysterious and undocumented, although Ben Hecht always claimed that Carl visited Petrograd in the summer of the Kerensky regime and also made contact in Stockholm with various Bolshevik leaders as they returned from exile. After the Bolshevik revolution he was entrusted by Borodin, whom he had known in Chicago as Axelrod, with a large sum of money to deliver to those Left Socialists in America who were already planning to found a Communist Party. When the ship arrived in New York he was taken off and questioned for a couple of days (there was yet no FBI) and the money was confiscated. Some say it was actually jewels, but clearer evidence is that it was $10,000 in a single bank draft. Whatever happened, we have letters from Sandburg substantiating the bare facts. This experience changed his life.

Sandburg's life changed as the life of Middle American man changed—as "The American Way of Life" became a slogan of petty businessmen's luncheon clubs. For many years it was the advertising slogan of the Buick car, often pictured parked under a tree with a happy, prosperous family enjoying a picnic on the lush grass in the clean countryside, and over it in great white letters, "The American Way of Life." In a famous photograph by Dorothea

49

Lange, strung across the foot of that sign was a bread line.

By the time of the Second World War, when Sandburg signed up with a large number of newspapers for a syndicated column, he had completely lost touch. The column was so sentimental and so blatantly patrioteering that one by one most of the papers dropped it. Meanwhile, of course, the orthodox Left Socialism in which Sandburg once believed had degenerated even more than he. He was no skilled economist, theoretician, or dialectician, and did not have to preserve his Socialism in the face of the Moscow Trials and the betrayals and murders of the Spanish Civil War. It had already gone.

"We had his youth." His youth was the youth of the century, the century that started out as the Century of Hope. No poet in any language expressed that hope better than Sandburg. And no poet was ever more completely the voice of the people. Hearing Sandburg read aloud "I Am the People, the Mob" was a very different experience from listening to the ceremonial magic of the rhythms of Whitman's revolutionary poems with their odd Quaker idioms, their misuse of French words, and their clumsy neologisms. Whitman wrote great poetry but he didn't learn it from his streetcar conductor and carpenter friends. Nobody ever talked that way. But Sandburg—everybody talked that way in our town, nobody knows why they don't anymore. Read the early poem "I Am the People, the Mob" and as much of the late book *The People, Yes* as you can. The answer is obvious. Sandburg's poetry has been translated into almost all civilized languages and he is the most popular American poet in the Third World, the Social Democratic countries, and even the People's Democracies. It is hard to understand why he never won the Nobel Prize when it was given to American writers like Sinclair Lewis and Pearl

Buck. He is by way of being an adopted national hero in Sweden.

Sandburg, like Whitman, turned out to be inimitable. Other people have written "like" him—Sherwood Anderson, Theodore Dreiser, Mike Gold, Herman Spector, Sol Funaroff, James Oppenheim, Lola Ridge, Kenneth Fearing, Kenneth Patchen, Allen Ginsberg, Lawrence Ferlinghetti, but they haven't written the same kind of verse. Whitman and Sandburg each tapped his own sources of a profoundly moving, a shaking, prosody which no one has ever discovered again. It is gone along with the America in which it was ordinary "interpersonal communication" raised to the highest power.

IV.

Is poetry correctly defined as interpersonal communication raised to the highest power? What do we mean by highest power? *"Sculpe! Limne! Cisle!"?* Intensity? Or scope? *Leaves of Grass? The Golden Bowl?* The classic American modernists, the people who are now taught in all respectable courses in modern American poetry, now the poetry of fifty years ago, chose intensity and deliberately abandoned scope, both of audience, and of meaning, or subject, or significance, and sought profundity in "An Egyptian Pulled Glass Bottle in the Shape of a Fish." What had happened? The moral collapse of which the First World War was more symptom than cause. What had happened was that thing called, fashionably, alienation, Toynbee's "schism in the soul," "secession of the elites." Whitman, the young Sandburg, were no more alienated than William Morris. It was their own society that they were trying to change. The future that they envisaged was an alternative, but it seemed to them a perfectly possible and praticable development of their past and their present. After the war few intellectuals in any part of the Western world believed in the existence of the Future in capital letters.

It is remarkable how narrow a base there was for the classic American modernists. A very few little magazines, *The Little Review, The Egoist, S4N, Others, The Double*

Dealer. The progressive editor of *Poetry* was Alice Corbin. After she married the painter Henderson and went to New Mexico, Harriet Monroe became increasingly resistive to the coaching of her foreign editor Ezra Pound, who transferred his powerful leverage to Margaret Anderson and *The Little Review*. William Marion Reedy stayed with the Populists, except for a little mild Expressionism to which he was introduced by his painter and sometime poet protégé— Albert Bloch, whom he was supporting in Munich. Then in 1920, *Reedy's Mirror* ceased publication, and it was the end of one strand of the German influence on the American avant-garde that had begun with Emerson and his friends, reached another peak with Sadakichi Hartmann and James Gibbons Huneker, another with *The Seven Arts,* and a final one with Ben Hecht and H. L. Mencken.

Conrad Aiken, Marianne Moore, Wallace Stevens, Mina Loy, Walter Conrad Arensberg, T. S. Eliot, William Carlos Williams appear all of them, altogether for the first time, in the magazine *Others* and in the *Others* anthologies. The editor was Alfred Kreymborg. No other editor in the whole history of twentieth-century American poetry was as open to radically new writing, and at the same time, as understanding and judicious.

It often seemed that Margaret Anderson believed that anything she couldn't understand must be art. What real discrimination the *Little Review* showed came largely from her associate, Jane Heap. *The Double Dealer* was certainly catholic in its tastes. It published, for instance, some of the earliest work of "Harold Hart Crane" and "Arthur Y. Winters" but it also published a lot of neo-Nineties and post-Lafcadio Hearn stuff of the sort that lingered on for generations in the provincial bohemia of New Orleans' French Quarter, as well as the writers of the new Southern

Renaissance, from William Faulkner to Allen Tate. *The Dial* published the avant-garde only after they became established and ceased to be avant of anything except the derrière-garde. *The Seven Arts* under James Oppenheim ceased toward the end of the War, or was absorbed by *The Dial*. It was the final expression of the Populist mystique which in the ruin of old values in the post-war world had become completely etherialized, but the group continued as a social circle, to merge with the group around the photographer Alfred Stieglitz. They were responsible for the big anthologies, *The American Caravan*, and finally for Dorothy Norman's *Twice a Year*. Waldo Frank, Hart Crane, Randolph Bourne, Lewis Mumford, and their friends believed in the mythic America of *Leaves of Grass* and *Huckleberry Finn* the way Plato believed in Athena and Apollo. Their best surviving spokesman is Lewis Mumford.

Kreymborg has never been given proper credit for the many years of hard work he devoted to the cause of the best American poetry. He was a minor poet himself and the first person except Vachel Lindsay to tour the country chanting his verses to music—to a mandolin-like instrument—something he said he invented and called a mandolute. The popularity of his act can be judged by the fact that some of his numbers were used in night clubs without permission by Jimmy Durante. Kreymborg sued. The judge, astonishingly, ruled for Durante, because, forsooth, poetry was by nature in the public domain. Kreymborg was not only the editor of *Others,* the magazine that was the turning point in American poetry, but one of the editors of Harold Loeb's *Broom,* certainly the best of all the avant-garde magazines, an editorial advisor of *The Seven Arts,* an editorial advisor of Alfred Stieglitz's *Camera*

Work, an editor of the *American Caravan* yearbooks, which were almost the last and finest effort of The Seven Arts Group, and finally an advisor of Dorothy Norman's when she started *Twice a Year,* the very last of all, far more mystic than Populist.

Kreymborg's *An Anthology of American Poetry* was incomparably the best of its period and his autobiography *Troubadour* is one of the most illuminating memoirs of the time. The only person he missed in *Others* was Gertrude Stein, probably because she didn't submit anything—*Tender Buttons* and similar little pieces do not seem to have been considered poetry in those days, even by herself. Later, in *Broom* and *The American Caravan* he amply made up for this oversight.

The history of art and literature is a sufficient answer to the social historians' attacks on the "great man theory of history." What would have happened if there had been no Ezra Pound, no Harriet Monroe, no William Marion Reedy, no Margaret Anderson, no Harriet Weaver, no Alfred Kreymborg? Would the baker's dozen of poets who have become American classics have forced their way into publication through other channels? I doubt it. Certainly they would not have been published by H. L. Mencken. Suppose they hadn't existed? Would the social and economic forces of American society have produced others like them to take their places? Would Maxwell Bodenheim or Skipwith Cannell or Jeanne D'Orge have filled the vacant spots and matured into major poets? Fifty per cent of them might have all died young at one Bloomsbury party, like Zola from a leaky coal stove. The base was narrow and the appeal was narrow, but as the meaning of life in the world between the wars grew ever narrower, the appeal widened.

T. S. Eliot was the representative poet of the time, for the same reason that Shakespeare and Pope were of their's. He articulated the mind of an epoch in words that seemed its most natural expression. Everything he said seemed to belong in some future edition of *Bartlett's Quotations*. He is the most difficult author in the twentieth century to avoid. Two generations of poets learned to write largely by carefully, year by year, shedding his influence, his metrics, his reading matter. When he gave up Jesse Weston's fertility cults for St. Thomas Aquinas and Anglican High Mass, thousands of young men and women all over the world followed him. The sermons of Lancelot Andrewes, to be found in the basements of most large secondhand bookshops, and easily purchased for a shilling or twenty-five cents a volume, became very expensive "collector's items."

The early poems have many virtues and the later poems may even be better, as they are certainly more profound poetry, but *The Waste Land* is the epic of *l'entre deux guerres*. Actually it is a philosophic revery—by no means an epic—and it establishes a type that was to be imitated in practically every civilized language. Scarcely a man is left alive who remembers that famous day and year. You have to have been there to know the impact of *The Waste Land*. It wasn't something in an English course. It was something in that very month's issue of *The Dial*, unprepared for, unexpected, overwhelming, also unannotated.

Eliot's earlier poems published in *Prufrock and Other Observations* in 1917 were not too startlingly out of the context of the general evolution of American verse. They had been preceded or paralleled by the poems of Donald Evans, Maxwell Bodenheim, and other not very good poets who deliberately imitated the bitter dandyism of Jules Laforgue. Laforgue's influence on American poetry is disproportionate to his importance in France. The reason for this is simple. Until recent years college courses in "Modern French Poetry" stopped with Laforgue and Verlaine—who were anything but modern. As a source of inspiration Verlaine had already been exhausted and debased by the Decadents, but even Laforgue came to most young American poets via Arthur Symons' sentimental *The Symbolist Movement in France* which softened Laforgue and, so to speak, Verlaine-ized him.

Pound was a tireless champion of Remy de Gourmont, both as critic and poet and so, in a different way, was John Gould Fletcher. The only other vital contact with French poetry was Jean de Bosschère who met all the American poets who visited London.

Wallace Stevens and Marianne Moore were more patently disciples of Jules Laforgue than anybody writing in French, and his influence in England on Edith Sitwell and the prose of Wyndham Lewis was determinative. (One of Laforgue's common devices was to describe people as though they were machines and machines and furniture as though they were alive, and landscapes as though they were chemicals.) Later in life Eliot was to claim that his early poems were inspired by Tristan Corbière and Alfred Jarry, but I suspect this of being a *post-facto* discovery. It is Laforgue's bitter, sarcastic, exiled clerk in his frayed cuffs and carefully blackened worn shoes who haunts the early poems, and J. Alfred Prufrock is Laforgue himself reborn, an exiled supernumerary out of contact, unable to achieve any significant human relationship, impossibly in love with a woman no less unobtainable for being so ordinary. In several poems there are direct echos of earlier French poets, especially of Théophile Gautier.

I know of no evidence that T. S. Eliot had ever read

Gottfried Benn until long after the First War, but Eliot's "evening sky stretched out like a patient etherized upon a table" is far more like Benn's early poems than it is like Laforgue, to whom it is usually compared, and Eliot's other poems of the city like "Rhapsody of a Windy Night" also resemble Benn's.

It is curious that America has never produced an important poet of the contemporary city, for all the frantic efforts of Harriet Monroe and other editors like her to promote such poetry. All they could ever find were popular magazine versifiers—John V. A. Weaver, for instance. Maxwell Bodenheim, who knew best and most of the underside of the modern city, wrote only doggerel, whether rhymed or free verse. Ezra Pound's "N.Y." is an artificial set piece that resembles a Norman Bel Geddes drawing. Carl Sandburg ceased to be able to write about Chicago after it became a "post-modern" city. Similarly, Eliot's London, like Benn's Berlin, is scarcely distinguishable from the Paris of Baudelaire, "lit with prostitutes," a smoky, gaslit city that was passing away before his eyes as he wrote. Of course London itself was an anachronism that lingered on until the Second World War. There are no poets of the contemporary American city until we get to Kenneth Fearing and Kenneth Patchen.

Very early Eliot begins to use literary cross-references, collages from the classics. Gautier's *"Carmen est maigre, —un trait de bistre / Cerne son oeil de gitana . . ."* turns into Eliot's Grishkin and puts on weight. But the poem "Whispers of Immortality" both echoes and refers to Webster and Donne and echoes Laforgue. "Gerontion," one of the best of the early poems, and with "The Love Song of J. Alfred Prufrock" and "Rhapsody of a Windy Night," one of the most definite forerunners of *The Waste Land,*

58

is made up almost entirely of echoes and of quotations, and is closely tied to a letter of Henry Adams to his brother written from Venice in a decaying season. Before Pound's *Cantos* Eliot was the first person in international literature to so consistently practice this extremely Alexandrian or late Roman method of making poetry out of tags and fragments of other peoples' verse, or, as in "Gerontion" and "The Journey of the Magi," prose (the latter poem is an anthology of bits from the Christmas sermons of Launcelot Andrewes).

It has become the custom in the most refined circles in literary America, even of the literary Left, to ignore the politics of Ezra Pound, T. S. Eliot, Wyndham Lewis, and D. H. Lawrence. But it would be a mistake to overlook the obvious fact of Eliot's anti-Semitism and the less obvious Sweeney poems, which, at the time Eliot wrote them, he certainly thought of as anti-Irish (besides paying off a much too rough boxing teacher).

Much has been made of Eliot's statement that he was a royalist, Anglo-Catholic, and classicist. Only Americans and profound eccentrics are royalists. Above the literary level of the illustrated weeklies The Family is only a boring joke in Great Britain. Eliot's Toryism was a politics out of what Australian aborigines call The Dream Time. He was not an Anglo-Catholic but a High Churchman, a very different thing indeed, and his knowledge of the English Church was so slight that he seriously suggested to the episcopacy of the Anglican communion, solemnly assembled in the palace of the Archbishop of Canterbury, that it behooved them to popularize from their pulpits the works of James Joyce. Long ago when I first read this I thought it was a joke, but indeed, it was not.

Of course Eliot was not a classicist, but a most extreme

spokesman of the romantic decadence. Like Paul Valéry, he adopted a neo-classicist esthetic from modern painting, and spoke of the poem as a completely depersonalized infernal machine carefully constructed by the dispassionate poet to explode in the reader's brain with all the fireworks of Clive Bell's "significant form." Like Valéry, Eliot banished the first-person singular from poetry, and persuaded all of his disciples and epigones to follow him. Behavior of this sort is a commonplace on the psychoanalytic couch and Eliot's poems, like Valéry's, have the embarrassing intimacy of the psychoanalytic confessional.

Certain symbols appear over and over again—someone looks out of the window on the spring garden where children are playing at sex in the lilac bushes; the pattern of the lymphatic system of the microcosm reflected in the pattern of the constellations in the macrocosm; Ezekiel's Valley of Dry Bones, Phlebas the Phoenician—the drowned sailor, the hanged man, the magician, and other figures in the Tarot pack, a strange game for a pious Anglo-Catholic; the incest conflicts and occult rituals of Shakespeare's *Tempest;* the virginal *Art nouveau* maiden, moist with dew, a child out of a repressed childhood; and over and over and over again that hackneyed trouble of the psychoanalytic patient, the fear of castration or impotence. It's all a little embarrassing. But that does not mean it is not great poetry. Most great poetry has been written from false principles and with covert, embarrassing, intimacy.

Once *The Waste Land* appeared it was possible to have seen it coming in the earlier poems, and as the years went by to see it dying away in *Ash Wednesday,* the choruses from *The Rock* and the *Four Quartets.* Some of the later minor

60

poems are probably leftovers from *The Waste Land* itself —which was once several times its final length. The earlier poems begin the method of radical dissociation and recombination of elements which culminate in *The Waste Land* and in Pound's *Cantos,* but at first they never advanced beyond Arthur Rimbaud's earliest uses of the method, as for instance in *Le Bateau ivre.* The elements of the poem are usually held together by an armature of narrative and mood much like Guillaume Apollinaire's "Zone." *The Waste Land* and the first *Cantos* push the technique to the point where it becomes a quite new method of composition.

It is common to trace this method to French poets after Baudelaire, to so-called Cubist poetry. There is a fundamental difference. Cubist poetry, say that of Pierre Reverdy, is like Cubist painting. There is one subject, a still life, the *Pont Neuf,* a girl with a guitar. The elements of that subject are broken up and dissociated both in space and time and recombined in a new, more esthetically powerful whole, but still the same subject. Pound, Eliot, and James Joyce in *Finnegans Wake,* did something very different. The subject is vague, ill-defined, grandiose, and appears as an after image of the collage of a wide variety of fragmentary subjects.

The Waste Land, like the *Cantos,* is full of bits of narrative and description and little dramas and elegies. Within itself each fragment is intact and is usually taken from somebody else's writing. The dissociated verbs and nouns, adjectives, and adverbs of Pierre Reverdy, Gertrude Stein, or Walter Arensberg are formed into new meanings. The collages of whole sentences and paragraphs of *The Waste Land* and the *Cantos* go to form new significances. The

61

first method, if such terms mean anything, is "classicist." The second, "romantic." The first is constructed, the second evocative. Both Eliot and Pound always claimed that they wrote in the first way but in fact, obviously, they wrote in the second.

Within a couple of years the influence of *The Waste Land* had become enormous, but only on the English-speaking literary bohemia. Soon little Waste Lands were sprouting everywhere. Nancy Cunard, Sam Beckett, Edgell Rickword, Raymond Larsson, Archibald MacLeish. *The Waste Land* became the literary Baedeker for Paris-America. It even influenced Ernest Hemingway. Even more outlandish and unexpected was its influence on Carl Sandburg, whose method in *The People, Yes* and *Good Morning, America,* is, after all, the same as that of the *Cantos* and *The Waste Land.*

Where did this method come from? It is not, like the Surrealist technique of free association, something anyone is likely to evolve naturally. Nor does it really resemble the Virgilian pastiches of Late Latin poetry which always "make sense" in a too ordinary fashion. Nor is it the "revolution of the word," the anti-Aristotelian attack on the presumptive syntax of the mind, of Eugene Jolas and the *surréalistes.* It seems to have been a discovery of Ezra Pound's and worked out in collaboration with Eliot over a very short period in the early Twenties. It does not derive from Apollinaire, whose associative method is much more fluent, far less disjunctive, a kind of half-controlled free association with an obvious "plot," and the same is true of the Apollinairian method of Blaise Cendrars' *La Prose du Transsibérien et de la Petite Jehanne de France.* In both the latter cases the technique derives from Whitman—improved by the movies. *The Cantos* and *The Waste Land* are put together like a collage still life by Juan Gris, but in which the cuttings from newspapers, playbills, theater tickets, and sheet music *are meant to be read*. Again the method is cinematographic but much more advanced. The analog is the later "ideological montage" of Sergei Eisenstein, in *Potemkin* and *Oktober*. As the years went by Eisenstein and Pound were mutually to influence one another. Although Eisenstein never dared to admit such an influence, he makes it obvious in an essay on Far Eastern poetry and the cinema which derives directly from Pound.

Eliot is certainly the most personal poet of the classic American modernists, more even than Conrad Aiken, whose intimacies have the remoteness of case histories. Eliot's case history is his own. But Pound really did write like Eliot claimed he wrote. In all of his work there is scarcely a glimmer of what philosophical jargon calls inter- and infra-subjectivity. The only personal poem about an "interpersonal" encounter is "The Villanelle of the Psychological Hour" and it is about an encounter which did not take place.

The Eliot-Aiken-Pound "Portraits of a Lady" are competitive set pieces—only Eliot's is about a real woman—and the purpose of the poems is not personal but literary. They are evaluations of Henry James's heroine. Their point is that in the post-War One world, the late Victorian and Edwardian woman of exquisite sensibility, refinement, graciousness, was at the end of her tether. There is no love poetry in Pound either. He even expurgates his Provençal translations, or misunderstands the obscure double meanings, and he ignores the pornography of two elegies of

Petronius. In one of his epigrams he says that he can't understand all the fuss about the twitching of a couple of abdominal nerves which only lasts for three minutes at the most. Yet he was married to one of the most famous beauties of pre-war literary England and a leading feminist to boot.

V.

WALLACE STEVENS, who began as the master Laforgian of them all, is full of people. Almost every poem in *Harmonium* is conceived as a brightly lit little drama. It's true that the figures are marionettes, or at the best, masks from the *commedia dell'arte*. When they both were young, Stevens and Edith Sitwell were often compared, and it is only necessary to compare them again to realize that Stevens' bright little people on his tiny crystalline stages are more than just personifications of his own problems, more than projections. The glass and painted tin and polished wood mannequins in Edith Sitwell's poems are not people at all, or even *dramatis personae*. They are simply moving visual *objects*—and auditory ones; they usually creak, or clack, or clatter. Reification is pushed to its ultimate. Stevens tirelessly quests the person or persons in the poem. They are exercises in I-Thou dialogue and always talk back to their creator. What Stevens usually says is that they speak an unknown tongue, perhaps unknowable. Stevens' characters have visions and the visions judge being.

Philosophizing poets have been a dime a dozen in our epoch but Stevens is the only one who is actually a philosopher. His philosophy is not the most profound in the world, and it is derivative. It bears great resemblance to George Santayana's "scepticism and animal faith," sometimes reversed—animalism and sceptic faith—with a dash of Josiah Royce—but it is far superior to all those people who have tried so hard to versify Marx or Whitehead or Wittgenstein.

Stevens' first book, *Harmonium,* did not have the sensational impact of *The Waste Land* or even the first ten *Cantos,* but many of us who read all three together, back in the days when the little toy dog was new, felt that there was "more to" *Harmonium,* that the insights were deeper, the judgments sounder, the vision clearer, and the metrics, above all, incomparably more sophisticated. Stevens seems to have risen to this height in one first leap, and could only thereafter fall away. As he grew older his poetry became more and more discursive and ruminative, and his prosody softer and more conventional. Philosophically he only worked out in informative discourse what had originally been far better presented in dramatic images, and imagined dramas of the mind.

Stevens is far less provincial than Eliot or Pound. They, like Ibsen, were provincial because they felt it necessary to lead a revolt against provincialism, and to educate the provincials.

The effectiveness of Eliot's critical essays is based on the assumption that his readers had never heard of Richard Crashaw or Bishop Bramhall or Lancelot Andrewes, and of course they had not, or his arguments would have fallen to pieces. Wallace Stevens takes it for granted that his readers are well-read, cultivated people who have recovered from the post-war disillusionment, abandoned both optimism and pessimism, and learned the un-American lesson that life is tragic—even if they are not aristocrats who absorb such wisdom with their mother's milk. He is what Nietzsche used to call a good European. Later in life he was to make friends with two of the last good Europeans, Ford Madox Ford and Léon-Paul Fargue. It is extraordinary how much the three men resemble one another in life attitudes, in what might be called the temper of the sensibility. Had all three wandered on to the stage of Ford Madox Ford's great novel *Parade's End,* they would have been quite at home in that atmosphere of over-civilized, ironic tragedy—but they'd have given it a happy ending, a very low-powered happy ending of scepticism and animal faith, just like in fact it has.

The test of Santayana is his poetry and his prose, his style. It wouldn't be of most philosophers, but his philosophy demands that it be judged by that criterion. So judged, Wallace Stevens is the greater philosopher. He is not a better philosopher in the technical sense, but he is far less rhetorical and sentimental. In fact he is not rhetorical and sentimental at all. Style is the judgment of the world, of being itself, in this philosophy.

This is Baudelaire's dandyism as an ontological principle. Baudelaire and Laforgue could never succeed as metaphysical dandyists, for the simple reason that their lives were too insecure and harried with poverty, sickness, or dissipation. Like an undevout astronomer, a squalid dandy is mad. Wallace Stevens was a successful executive of a business which in his day was still a gentlemanly profession. He could afford a distinguished air, and afford to make a success of it. Most dandies have been ragamuffins, more pitiful than tragic. They may have been great poets like Baudelaire or historically significant ones like Laforgue or Oscar Wilde, but the strange malice with which they distorted the world was too often embarrassing. In American poets like Donald Evans and Maxwell Bodenheim it always was. The very point of Wallace Stevens' dandyism is, that although constructed entirely of tragic irony and the most acute sensibility, it is impossible for it ever to embarrass anyone.

If the mind can be so constructed, the sensitivity so attuned, principle so unfalteringly adhered to, it is quite possible to produce poetry in which there are no mistakes. This does not mean that the verse of Wallace Stevens should be a model for others; it should not, for that very reason. It is the achievement of an individual poet as a unique being—a style.

Back in the days when they first appeared, Marianne Moore seemed a kind of lesser Wallace Stevens with more detail and less brains. But Wallace Stevens was about things, people, events, emotions, realized via persons. There is even an undercurrent of general ideas. Marianne Moore confined herself to things, and took from Henry James the guiding principle that the artist should be totally inaccessible to the commonplace emotions. The word "precious" is usually a term of condemnation. For Marianne Moore it is the highest possible praise. Life itself is seen as "An Egyptian Pulled Glass Bottle in the Shape of a Fish" and she does not permit it to be seen in any other way. She, like Stevens, has often been compared to Edith Sitwell, but Edith Sitwell's bric-a-brac universe is a form of rather savage metaphysical sarcasm. Marianne Moore approves of hers. She not only likes it that way but she is incapable of seeing it otherwise. This in itself is an ironic and witty commentary on the world as it really is. It even has a scarcely audible note of tragedy, but it's doubtful if that is intentional. I've often wondered if Tennessee Williams got the idea and the title for his play, *The Glass Menagerie,* from the contemplation of Marianne Moore and her poetry. Certainly the play could stand as a perfect criticism of both person and poems.

What was startling about Marianne Moore's verse when it first appeared was its prosody. We did not know then that it was almost entirely collage. Poem after poem is made up of National Park Service Bulletins, advertising copy, travelogues, bits of novels, the endless flow of printed matter in which the modern mind is forced to swim. All this prose was measured off in lines of syllabic verse (that is, syllables, not accents, are counted, and there are no metrical feet as in accentual and quantitative verse). These lines are read as strophes and since they end in the most outrageous places, the prosody itself creates an extraordinarily ironic wit, as delicate as it is sharp. Since lines are long and filled with detail, the delicacy is not at first apparent, but in fact, although Marianne Moore too has been called a Laforgian, the real resemblance is to Emily Dickinson.

Other women of her generation, notably Elinor Wylie, tried to claim the heritage of Emily Dickinson, but today their verses seem thin stuff indeed, while Marianne Moore's survives. More apparently inhuman poetry has probably never been written. What makes its inhumanity so pointed is its obvious function as a mask, but what does it mask? Emily Dickinson's nunlike life and ascetic verse protect a sensibility so fragile and so sharp that life out in the world, struggling with the flesh and the devil, would have destroyed it instantly, and what little of the world did penetrate in the cloister wounded, crippled and eventually destroyed her.

There is a progression in the development of a carapace for the sensibility. Emily Brontë, Christina Rossetti, Emily Dickinson, Marianne Moore. They all write about the same thing, the vertigo of the sensibility in a world of terror. As the world becomes more terrible with the progress of Western Civilization, the protective armor grows at the expense of the dweller within. Until, with Marianne Moore, the living being is hard to find; that is what the poems say and that is why they are tragic. If they said only "Look at me, how exquisitely sensitive I am!" they would be sentimental kitsch. Sentimental they are, but there is a good sentimentality as well as a bad. Made up of almost entirely other people's writing and almost all of them people of no literary importance whatsoever, her poems, one would expect, should be utterly impersonal. On the contrary they are totally personal—the peculiar and peculiarly distorted expression of a unique person, or rather of one person's uniqueness, which is why of all the classic American modernists, Marianne Moore has never had any disciples or even occasional imitators.

Collage, found sculpture, accident, do not depersonalize art. Nothing in the world looks like a Kurt Schwitters collage except another Kurt Schwitters collage. So with "accidental art"—Hans Arp or Marcel Duchamp and all their latter-day imitators. What influence Marianne Moore has had has been prosodic. To her can be traced the distortion of natural rhythms and concealment of strophic lines in strictly measured pseudo-metric, a technique employed by several later poets, notably James Laughlin, who certainly otherwise do not resemble Marianne Moore.

For many years the lost member of the classic modernists was Mina Loy. Partly this was due to change of taste. The Proletarians, the Metaphysicals, and the Reactionary Generation had no use for her free verse, her bawdiness, and her lack of gravity. A clever critic manipulating texts could demonstrate that Pound, Eliot, Williams, Aiken, Stevens were all socially responsible. Marianne Moore, like a piece of precious bric-a-brac, had got herself wedged into a literary ecological niche and refused to be budged. Mina Loy

70

was like those kings whom history has always given a bad press because no party wanted to claim them. The years of economic crisis, preparation for war, and World War Two did not provide a congenial climate for Mina Loy's reputation.

Today things have changed. She has been rediscovered and when the present generation—the counter culture—can find her poems, they are read with enthusiasm. Hundreds of people in little magazines and in the underground press who have never heard of her, and never will, write like her, but not nearly so well. She was the only poet of this group who wrote frankly erotic verse. All the rest, except Aiken, are distinguished by their sexlessness, and every critic and anthologist of the period has held Aiken's dreamy eroticism against him. On the other hand she bears no resemblance whatever to the vertiginous lady love poets of the Edna Millay school, nor to the lonely Greenwich Village maidens and Middle Western women in rut who wrote for Joe Kling's *Pagan,* the outstanding organ of erotic verse in the Twenties, nor does her extremely sophisticated free verse bear any resemblance to any other American's.

Mina Loy grew up as a young writer in Europe and her verse is more like that of some of the Dadaists, notably Philippe Soupault in French, or August Stramm, the German Futurist. For a while she was married to the boxer Arthur Craven, a poet and one-man happening, who was a mythic figure of the great days of Dada. Mina Loy's verse read with the eye seems random and jerky. Read aloud with any sensitivity to its rhythms it is apparent that it is a new prosodic development, at least for English.

Perhaps one reason for the waning of Mina Loy's reputation (Pound at one time preferred her to Marianne Moore) is that she did not really belong in the group I have called

71

the classic American modernists but with those poets who were the American representatives of the international avant-garde of the time, Gertrude Stein, Walter Conrad Arensberg, and, ten years later, Laura Riding and Eugene Jolas. Gertrude Stein and Walter Arensberg were writing Cubist poetry, strictly so called, before the leading Cubist poet, Pierre Reverdy, had perfected his style. Poems like "Susie Asado," some of *Scenes,* some of *Tender Buttons,* are the most perfect things of their kind ever written. The kind is not major poetry, but then, the still lifes of Chardin and Juan Gris are not the Sistine Chapel, either.

Arensberg was by way of being a great amateur, a gentleman of letters, a patron of the arts, a friend of Francis Picabia and Marcel Duchamp, and their host when they came to America in the war years, the subsidizer of their magazine *Wrong-rong,* which introduced Dadism to New York. (Ben Hecht introduced it to Chicago.) Most of his earlier poetry sounds as though it had been translated from the French, and moves from a Verlainian lyricism to the much anthologized Mallarméan "Voyage à l'infini." Suddenly in the last numbers of *Others* he began to publish Cubist verse much like Gertrude Stein's *Tender Buttons* but less impersonal, and then strange, Futurist-Dadaist poems that resemble the printing on the ironic pseudo-electrical schematics and mechanical drawings of Francis Picabia. The latter are classics, illustrated in all histories of modern art; the rather better poems of Arensberg are forgotten. Arensberg stopped publishing poetry and spent an immense amount of money decoding Bacon out of Shakespeare and collecting modern art. The Arensberg Collection in Philadelphia is the best for its period in the world and contains, incidentally, almost all the known work of Marcel Duchamp.

Most of the rest of the *Others* group do not stand the

72

test of rereading after half a century. Although read as a whole, the file of the magazine and the three anthologies recreate the literary moods, the intellectual climate, the conversations and enthusiasms of those days, and provide a context for the major figures who have become classics. Skipwith Cannell, Jeanne D'Orge, are simply not good poets. A possible exception is Evelyn Scott, who somehow just failed of being a very important writer. Her novels, poems, and autobiography and book of memories of Tennessee at the turn of the century are all still readable. She was certainly the best avowedly feminist poet of her time and one of the first of the later much publicized Southern Renaissance. Perhaps that is what is wrong. Although she seems to have known almost everybody of the international bohemia of her day, she was just a little too early to find a context in which she could develop what she uniquely had to say. Her contemporaries, writers and publishers, respected her, in fact were a little afraid of her powerful personality. She had little trouble getting published and appears as late as the *American Caravans* of the Thirties. She published some sixteen or more books but almost all of them were remaindered—(but then almost the whole of the first edition of Wallace Stevens's *Harmonium* was remaindered. I bought two hundred copies at 18¢ a copy and gave all except one away). The South, which is so proud of its writers, should see to her resurrection, and she should be popular with the literary spokeswomen of Women's Liberation, for her mature, forthright, hard verse is far better than that of the lady poets and better than any verse by a feminist until Laura Riding. (Mina Loy, Marianne Moore, Amy Lowell are neither feminists nor lady poets . . .)

Marsden Hartley, another one of the *Others* group, studied painting in Germany and was one of the most advanced Expressionists. In those days he wrote poetry of a similar character. Later on, back in America, both his poetry and painting changed to become simple, direct, painfully honest, unabashedly personal. Another *Other* was Wallace Gould, a great favorite of Kreymborg, Stevens, and William Carlos Williams and now forgotten. He was a recluse, originally from Maine, and a friend of Hartley's, who seldom left his home in a small Virginia town, and who wrote again simple personal poetry in a long, free-verse line, peculiar to himself, and perfectly fitted to the sadness, and nostalgia, and renunciation of the world that saturate his verse. There is no one quite like Gould in American poetry. He resembles Harold Munro a little, but differs in the use of a long, Gregorian line that chants itself, and he's a little like Francis Jammes, but Jammes was one of the happiest men ever to write poetry and Gould is always genuinely a man of sorrows.

VI.

THIS leaves William Carlos Williams, the greatest of the group and the only one whose influence has lasted until this day, has not only lasted, but has grown, until it surpasses that of T. S. Eliot in the years between the wars. Before going on to Williams, the bridge to the future, there are some people who have been left over—Gertrude Stein, of whom I already have said almost enough. The important thing to understand about Gertrude Stein is that she is nowhere near as deep as she seems. She always said she meant literally whatever she said, and indeed she did. No one in any language has made more profound direct studies in the practice of literature of the syntax of the mind, the psychology of communication. She belongs with the American anthropologists and philologists who have made the most radical studies of language, with Edward Sapir and Whorf—both of whom incidentally were fair poets. In her salad days it was almost impossible to convince anybody that her work should be taken literally, that there was nothing mysterious behind it. Late in life she became a celebrity and started to "talk sense" and revealed herself as a person of commonplace intellect and childlike general ideas. None the less some of her early poems are amongst the finest things of their period—Tennyson had a commonplace mind, too.

Emmanuel Carnevali was an innocent, what Wyndham Lewis, in rejecting his own youth, was to call "a revolutionary simpleton," a simple, naïve, intensely passionate man. He blossomed as a poet in Chicago and his verse, like Robert MacAlmon's, is in style a last flareup of Midwestern Populism; but it is not socially oriented, but directly, shamelessly personal. After a few years as a character in the bohemia of Chicago and New York he became chronically ill, with what was finally diagnosed as Parkinson's disease, and went home to Italy to a long drawn-out dying, to loneliness and poverty, relieved only by correspondence with his old friends.

If ever there was a one man or one woman happening, it was the Baroness Elsa von Freitag-Loringhofen, possesor of one of the most aristocratic of German names. She appeared out of nowhere in *The Little Review* office with a sheaf of poems, the like of which Margaret Anderson and Jane Heap had never seen or dreamed of. They were written in Teutonic pigeon English and they were a deliberate embrace of madness, not Rimbaud's reasoned derangement of the senses, but simply derangement. Her verse represented a far more radical revolt against reality than Stramm or Kurt Schwitters or Tristan Tzara. She was the perfect expression of immediate post-war Rhineland Dadaism, but it is open to question if she had ever heard anything about it until she came to America and met Marcel Duchamp. She wrote an immense amount of poetry, comparatively little of which ever saw print, and some of which, it is to be hoped, will be turned up some day from the various university libraries' special collections of the papers of magazines and individuals of the time. What was printed was extraordinary enough. There is a very amusing discussion between Jane Heap and Evelyn Scott of her work reprinted in *The Little Review Anthology*. Not until the later days of the Surrealist movement would there be so good a discussion of art as willed madness, conscious *Kranken-kunst*. The Baroness Elsa intrudes a short comment in which she quotes Goethe: *"Nur wer die Sehnsucht kennt —weiss was ich leide"* and continues, "Haven't all high-cultured emotional people (as even as a public custom— in old Greece, in the feast of Dionysus) to be insane for a time—like the steam nozzle on teakettle? *Because Ameri-cans do not need that—they should not give costume balls!"*

The Baroness went to costume balls at Webster Hall in Greenwich Village and the Dill Pickle on Chicago's Near North Side naked, her head shaved and painted green, her body decorated with postage stamps (which she commonly wore on her face instead of beauty spots) and with a girdle of kitchen utensils. She saw William Carlos Williams' car parked outside a Greenwich Village tearoom, climbed in, took off her clothes, and waited. She made innumerable constructions of junk sculpture and collages of rubbish. She smoked marijuana in a big china German pipe that must have held half an ounce or more. She was arrested several times and at last committed, and I believe deported. She returned to the Rhineland and died in great poverty, ostra-cized by her family, unknown to the German artists and writers like her, selling newspapers on the winter streets. One world war produced the Baroness; the second world war produced thousands of Baronesses all over the world. Long ago when I was very young I asked Marcel Duchamp, "Would you call the Baroness a Futurist or a Dadaist?" He replied, "She is not a Futurist. She is the future."

We return to William Carlos Williams. A dying social order, a dead language, a value system emptied of mean-ing—to assault the Old World with the learned arrogance

77

of T. S. Eliot or the willed madness of the Baroness is to assault it with pride, and pride goeth before a fall. William Carlos Williams subverted it with humility. He has been a Taoist revolutionary—"Water seeks always the lowest place and washes away mountains."

T. S. Eliot's objective correlative—"a set of objects, a situation, a chain of events which present like a miniature drama the emotions, ideas, the judgments of a poet without comment"—becomes in William Carlos Williams "no ideas except in things," not a *reductio ad absurdum,* least of all a childish misunderstanding of Locke and Hume, not a philosophical principle at all, *but a method for constructing a poem.* The famous plums in the icebox embody a poem of married love about which nothing whatever is said. *The Waste Land* and the *Cantos* are elaborately constructed denunciations of the false values of a predatory society, in which symbolism and objective correlative slip into rhetoric. Williams never slips. The symbolic drama of "To Elsie" begins with flat statement, "The pure products of America / go crazy" and ends, "No one / to witness / and adjust, no one to drive the car."

Mostly it's not a matter of correlative at all, which after all is just Symbolism toughened up. It's just objective. Finally of course the meaning is that the transcendent and the immanent are not somewhere else. They are the thing itself, not the thing *in* itself, no occult *Ding an Sich,* just itself. The Sacrament is the bread and wine. It was not until the great popularity of Zen Buddhism that Williams' "message" would become generally comprehensible. "Wholeness, harmony, and radiance" need only to be pointed to in the ordinary. Williams always thought of himself as a secularist of secularists, as totally anti-mystical. At least that's what he always said.

Williams was the master of the put-on. He used to tell people that *Kora in Hell* was a collection of notes he'd taken on his grandmother's conversation, when of course it is a kind of parody of the *Vita Nuova* of Dante. In his later years he went around on the college poetry-reading circuit telling the professors and the students that he had made a revolutionary prosodic discovery, the expandable foot in which you could have as many syllables or accents as you wished. Everybody took notes and Bill's prehensile foot has become a standard tool of academic exegesis.

Back to Williams as visionary. There is no difference really between his crystalline reductions of sensory awareness and Francis Thompson's "Turn but a stone and start a wing / 'Tis you, 'tis your estrangéd faces / That miss the many splendored thing!" except that Williams is a better poet and doesn't talk about experience; he reveals it with humility. Presumably this is what Gertrude Stein hoped to do in *Tender Buttons*. Alas those still lifes, however excellent in their way, are the work of an apothecary and will go down in history for their purely formal virtues as perfect literary exemplifications of analytical Cubism. No one would ever think of saying such things about Williams. Little epigrams of objective vision, the red wheelbarrow, the locust tree in flower, the cat in the jam closet, the young woman at the window, the great figure 5 on the fire truck, the young proletarian woman with a nail in her shoe— there's been nothing quite like these poems since the epitaphs for grasshoppers and the epigrams accompanying the gift of a courtesan's comb to Aphrodite in the Greek anthology.

Williams had a far better education than he pretended, and was not as unaware of his pure classicism as he claimed. Classicism as an art movement of course is a late form of Romanticism, assuming that Romanticism as an art movement goes back to the beginning of the Baroque. Williams is not at all a "Classicist." He simply writes like Homer or Sappho. It's not for nothing that Matthew Arnold picked Homer's watchfires before the walls of soon to be destroyed Troy as a touchstone. He was right; that is the way the best poetry is written, and if sharp little scenes in a German Easter egg like this are properly called Homeric visions, Williams is a most Homeric writer.

There is a decided difference between the classicism of H.D. and that of Williams. However poignant the imagism of H.D., the poems owe so much of their piercing quality to the romanticizing reference to their Greek subjects. The Greeks when they wrote poetry had no emotional cross-references to the Cretans or the Egyptians. Williams likewise has no cross-references. The poem is the self-contained classic experience. The poetic situation is uncontaminated, and therefore unromanticized. The dichotomy, form and content, is an abstraction.

Williams is the greatest prosodist of his generation because he is the greatest poet. Perhaps he really did believe in prehensile feet, and worked entirely by ear, but it's extremely doubtful. A lifetime spent as a doctor, especially a pediatrician handling troubled mothers, had taught him a certain canniness and subterfuge in dealing with the will to delusion. Whitman's ceremonial chant, Sandburg's folk speech, Ezra Pound's echoes of the Latin hexameter and elegiac distich, H.D.'s strophic imitations of the choruses of Euripides, Goethe, Hölderin, Matthew Arnold, the sprung rhythms of Gerard Manley Hopkins and Robert Bridges, the *vers libre* of Vielé-Griffin and the different free verse of the generation after Apollinaire, all these explorations are pulled together and synthesized by Williams.

Again, it should be pointed out parenthetically that Williams was far better read in other languages than English than he pretended to be. He translated his friend Philippe Soupault's *Last Nights of Paris,* but in later years he always claimed that he didn't translate it at all, he just helped Philippe with a few American idioms. A comparison of the two book shows immediately how false this is. Similarly, to people who didn't know any better, he would commonly deny any knowledge of French or German, although he studied abroad, both as a boy and as a young doctor; or that he knew either Latin or Greek, although we have evidence to the contrary in his letters to H.D. All this is part of his conception of himself as the leader of "Anti-literature." There is only one influential modern prosody that he scrupulously avoids, the decadent iambic pentameter of Jacobean and early Caroline drama which essentially is the verse form of almost all of T. S. Eliot's poetry.

Eliot himself has said that no matter how putatively free the verse, there is always a reference to the five-foot, five-accent, ten-syllable line—the natural form for English speech. English maybe, says Williams, but not American, and not in the twentieth century. The iambic pentameter is exhausted even as distorted and sprung in *The Tempest* or in Webster, Ford, or Shirley, or Gerard Manley Hopkins or Robert Bridges. Early poems of Williams in long lines, "The Wanderer" for instance, look like that's what they were—but read "The Wanderer" aloud. There are two ten-syllable lines in the first fifteen. The source, if you listen carefully, is Swinburne's "Sapphics," a poem every poet of Williams' generation knew by heart. We have forgotten the powerful stimulus to prosodic freedom—"All the night Sleep came not upon mine eyelids / Shed not dew nor shook nor unclosed a feather / Yet with lips shut tight and

81

with eyes of iron, / Stood and beheld me." Even the subject is the same. Artemis or Aphrodite driving the mystes to vision—"Out into the deserted streets of Paterson." The young Williams was at least as much a Hellenist as H.D. He just transposed the Doric mode to a strictly American music. This incidentally, to take the metaphor literally, is precisely what blues does. The blues chord progression is a subtly altered Doric mode.

In his earliest verse Williams constantly uses the irregular caesura, the multiple caesura, and the runover line; lines that end in "the," "of," "and," "with," "but," fascinate him. What he is after is a strophe that breaks the syntax and creates an anti-logic, an anti-rational wit which finds a new rationality, and a new logic—Gertrude Stein, André Breton, Korzybski, Norbert Weiner, Whorf—the effort to free the thought processes of modern man living in a polyvalent, polymorphous, multiphasic universe opened up by his technology, from the Euclidian patterns of Aristotelian logic based on an idealization of Greek grammar and syntax. This becomes a battle cry of poets, logicians, philologists, psychiatrists, and all sorts of people as the twentieth century grows old.

Williams' attack is not as obvious or as thorough-going as Pierre Reverdy's or Gertrude Stein's but it is more subtle and it is sufficient. Step by step Williams' disciples—Louis Zukovsky, Charles Olson, Robert Creeley—were to push the anti-logic of his prosody further and further until at last they get something like the most extreme epigrams of the sensibility, untranslatable Japanese *waka* or Mallarmé's "Petit air."

In *Paterson,* Williams takes over from Pound and Marianne Moore the collage of extended materials; long passages of slightly altered prose, letters, and documents, and combines them with all the poetic forms he had developed in a lifetime of exploration. *Spring and All* and *Kora in Hell,* snapshots like "The Attic Which Is Desire," written in the heyday of American modernism, are forecasts of *Paterson,* but they are only fragmentary anticipations. *Paterson* is an extraordinary synthesis, a profoundly personal portrait of a man as the nexus of a community, which expands out from him and contracts into him like the ripples from a cast stone moving in both directions simultaneously. It is also what we used to call a philosophical epic, but it is not a revery like Zukofsky's *A* but a dramatic narrative. Also it is distinguished by its high degree of integration. The very subject of *The Waste Land* is disintegration. Pound's original plot for the *Cantos* disintegrates with his mind. *A* and *Maximus* can only end with their authors. Williams went on writing *Paterson* to the end of his life, but the poem has a beginning, a middle, and a long ending cadence, and it really is a philosophical epic, although its overt philosophizing is rather childlike. Its implicit philosophy, the pedal point that sustains all its manifold melodies and recitativas, is a profound philosophy indeed—"It is the thing itself which is transcendent."

There is a widely held belief that Williams was not appreciated by his peers until late in his life. Who were his peers? Certainly the classic American modernists. Each thought Williams was the second greatest American poet, the first of course being himself. Except Eliot, who detested him, a feeling Williams reciprocated. The minor poets of the period, the contributors to *Others, The Little Review,* and *Broom,* were all deeply influenced by him, and from then on, hundreds of forgotten contributors to little magazines imitated him. He became the leader of underground poetry when the Proletarians, and after them, the Reactionary Generation, had formed an impenetrable "crust of custom" over the surface of American literature, obscuring everything that went on in the depths. After the Second War, as they became discredited, and then forgotten, Williams emerged both to write his best poetry and to be the acknowledged leader of the young. He is the only one of his contemporaries of whom this is true . . . except for Pound who was admired for non-literary reasons—because he got in trouble with the government and was opposed to the war—no matter why.

There is an extra-literary reason for Williams' influence, too. By and large, writers are not very nice people. Most of them are quarrelsome, vindictive, malicious. There are too many piglets, and too little swill in the trough, so there is a good deal of squealing and backbiting. American writers have a fixed idea that they are not welcome in their society and this makes them arrogant. Williams was a very nice man. Friendly, modest, always ready to extend a helping hand, yet never given to ballyhooing his disciples, like Pound, although he was lavish and perhaps indiscriminate in praise and encouragement. I once met Parker Tyler walking on clouds down Eighth Street. "I just got a letter from Bill," said he. "He says *The Granite Butterfly* is as great as Dante." "Hell," said I, "that ain't nothing. He compared me to Homer," and he was quite likely to compare the desperate doggerel of a sex-starved housewife claustrated in the American purdah to the poems of Sappho. Williams' attitude seems to have been a combination of a Franciscan universal sympathy and "You never can tell, with a little encouragement to the unrepossessing sprouts, genius might grow and flower," and so it did in many cases.

VII.

THE people we have been discussing were not products of the First War; they were formed in the first fifteen years of the century, those dreamy Edwardian days when progress seemed, at least to its beneficiaries, to be reaching its zenith; when, to the outsiders, a new, just, and sane social order seemed just around the corner, when everyone anyone knew had beautiful manners, and when it was possible to quote seriously Walter Pater's "gemlike flame," and Arthur Symons' "I burn that all may see Beauty." A world so like its last three months of life in that halcyon balmy summer of 1914 which ended with screaming crowds on packed trains fleeing from their long vacations. The war shattered or killed or irrevocably changed the modernist generation. It formed the next. Sandburg's letters, Richard Aldington's, William Carlos Williams', Alfred Kreymborg's, Conrad Aiken's autobiographies speak out of a different world from Malcolm Cowley's *Exile's Return* or Robert McAlmon's *Being Geniuses Together*.

e. e. cummings' *The Enormous Room* is the first record outside of Russia of an intellectual in a concentration camp, locked up by a bureaucracy out of Kafka for no apparent reason except that they didn't like his looks. It didn't matter that he was a volunteer ambulance driver for the French Army; that only made it worse. Aldington, Herbert Read,

85

Robert Graves, Ford Madox Ford—they had the experiences of mud, blood, lice, and tears, but the new factor, as is obvious in all the books about the First War, is the true horror that was unmasked between 1914 and 1924—the realization that, under the surface of progress and high culture, Western Civilization had matured a militantly mindless and murderous bureaucracy which was now breaking through the ornamented façade and taking over. *The Enormous Room* was the experience of only a few, but it was not exceptional; it was prognostic. A generation later it would be the experience of millions and it would be pushed from its mild beginnings to its final conclusion, to the Final Solution of the Nazis. This is the difference. For the post-war generation, the quality of experience and the meaning of life have been altered irrevocably; Graves, Eliot, Herbert Read, and the rest challenged that experience with the old values. The new generation started raw, with the new quality of life as primary.

As has often been remarked, e.e. cummings is not as "modernistic" as he looks on paper. In his earliest verse he is adolescent, kittenish, Swinburnian. The Swinburnianism slowly dies away and then the kittenism, but the adolescence remains throughout his life. The moral catastrophe of the war froze him in his own youth. Faced with what the Establishment means by the real world, he simply refused to grow up. His typographical capers have been compared to the *Calligrammes* of Guillaume Apollinaire, but Apollinaire's pictorial printing is the amusement of an overmature man. cummings used typography to break up sound and meaning, a very different and more serious, or more seriously comic, thing than printing poetry about rain in vertical streaming lines. cummings introduces clowning into the shamelessly sentimental contexts of the poems. This kind of self-conscious defense is of course itself adolescent. But there's good sentiment and bad sentiment and there's nothing wrong with adolescence.

e. e. cummings grew up reading those revolutionary pamphlets, the Oz books, in which children and their toys run society and run it far better than adults do, off there in the Real World beyond the Deadly Desert—which can only be crossed by magic. cummings is the poet laureate of Oz, but an Oz which has become a garrison society and beyond which lies only the world of *The Castle* and *The Trial*.

Past the middle of the century that land of youth would break out of its garrison and make a bid to become an alternative society. Not only would cummings become very popular, but his sentimental poems, which seemed so unreal, would come to reflect the common human relationships of the youth culture.

It's so simple. cummings has often been compared to Apollinaire and to Francis Carco and later to Raymond Queneau and Jacques Prévert. All right, compare him. They are all what orchardists call trees past their full bearing, "post-mature." Carco is sentimental enough, but part of the sentimentality is an all-pervasive world weariness. Compare Pierre MacOrlan's poems about prostitutes to cummings' sonnets on the same subject, which some people consider his best work. MacOrlan's whores are real whores, friends with whom he has discussed everything there ever was over a Byrrh and a Pernod. cummings' are the wonderful creatures encountered by a Harvard boy on his visits to the wicked stews of Boston. There is nothing Marxist or Christian or any other philosophical objection to war in his antiwar poems; he just thinks it stinks and in the final analysis is fomented by nasty old ladies on Brattle Street and cigar-smoking Babbitts from downtown.

There's nothing wrong with this; it's perfectly sound judgment, sounder in many ways than a treatise on the falling rate of profit and the necessity of an economy of permanent war.

As cummings grew older he grew more and more harassed and embittered by the unbelievable folly of the world. He was crippled and in constant pain with arthritis and he became a crank. He is responsible for some of the most vicious anti-Semitic verse ever written by an important poet, surpassing even Ezra Pound. Fortunately for his reputation, his publishers have expurgated this stuff from his collected editions.

The real trouble with cummings is that he isn't terribly good. Go back and read the "Epithalamium" which opens *Tulips and Chimneys* (which, with *is 5,* is probably one of his two best books). Is "Epithalamium" a put on? Could anybody seriously print such stuff? Yet he could write lovely boyish love songs with all the pathos of time's winged chariot hurrying down Eighth Street in Greenwich Village. On the other hand he could also write some dreadfully kittenish pornography which is positively bad girlish. How infantile cummings' pornography sounds alongside Eliot's "King Bolo and His African Queen" or Auden's "The Platonic Blow" or Henry Reed's hilarious parodies of A. E. Housman or Bob Brown's great Oxbridge and Camford limericks which have passed into folklore. cummings' pornographic poems are embarrassing, like dirty jokes told at Ozma's birthday party.

cummings was one of the first Paris Americans on the scene, not long after Mina Loy. But from the demobilization of the First War to the outbreak of the World Economic Crisis in 1929 the Café Dome became the capitol of the English-speaking avant-garde. Everybody who was anybody could be found within a short walk of the corner of the Boulevard Raspail and the Boulevard Montparnasse, getting drunk in the Select, the Rotonde, the Dome, the Jockey, the Dingo, the Vikings, the Negre de Toulouse. As news of this concentration of genius got abroad, all summer long the corner swarmed with crowds of students and middle-aged tourists, come to peep at the great. After midnight the painter Ortiz broke up the glassware at the Dome and Bob McAlmon got in fights at the Select and the American painter Hilaire Hiler played whorehouse jazz and ragtime on the piano at the Jockey—whose walls were decorated with his own Cubist paintings of redskins—while Les Copeland, the first and greatest Western folksinger, sang Joe Hill's "Shall we be slaves and work for wages / It is outrageous / Has been for ages . . ." to the tune of "Red Wing." College girls fainted at the sight of James Joyce drowsing over a gin in the Rotonde or Gertrude Stein shopping for *primures et vollailles* in the street market in the center of Boulevard Raspail. Everybody knew everybody else because there were only a few hundred people in the world. Ilya Ehrenberg met Louis Aragon and Louis Aragon met Nancy Cunard and Nancy Cunard met Sam Beckett and Sam Beckett met Harold Loeb, the publisher of *Broom* who knocked Hemingway out on a beach in Spain in a quarrel over a drunken slut.

Broom and *Secession* were the best magazines of the period, and they were directly the products of the post-war world. They, like the immigration itself, were brought into being by *voluta,* by the difference between the hard American dollar and the inflated paper currencies of bankrupt Europe. *Broom* is probably the best magazine of literature and the arts ever published by an American. Lola Ridge, Alfred Kreymborg, Frances Midner, Malcolm Cowley,

Matthew Josephson, all had a hand in editing it. Until Cowley and Josephson took over and brought it back to America, it owed its uniformly high quality, catholicity, and maturity of taste to the editorial genius of Harold Loeb himself. It was never stuffy and correct like *The Dial* or hysterical and uncritical like *The Little Review*. Until the Surrealists managed to drum up money from millionairesses and art dealers to finance magazines like *Documents* and *Minotaure, Broom* was the best avant-garde magazine in any language, and that includes the sumptuous Russian ones of those days, or the handsome magazines produced by the German Expressionists, and later the Constructivists and Suprematists.

Those were the days of the famous Lost Generation, the "expatriates." There wasn't anything particularly lost or expatriate about them. Most of them were well off to begin with, had a vacation for a couple of years in Europe, and went back to successful careers in America. For Lost read alcoholic. For expatriates read tourists. They lived abroad for two reasons: the power of the dollar over the runaway currency inflation in Europe, and the prohibition of alcoholic drinks in America. The fact that they were abroad seems to have obsessed them. They thought of themselves as exiles and they were continuously attacked by the American Establishment, and in fact often still are today, because they were living abroad. They felt guilty about it, and wrote patriotic books like Malcolm Cowley's *Exile's Return* and Archibald MacLeish's *New Found Land*.

Although they bought drinks in the Dôme and Rotonde for most of the leading personalities of the European avant-garde, the contemporary revolutions in European art, letters, and politics scarcely touched most of them. It was considered bourgeois to go to galleries and utterly demented to go to the Louvre and few of them read French for pleasure and spoke very little. The ordinary French people and the cops on Montparnasse called them *ou ests* —"ooh ay lee cafey Dome?" *Broom* published many of these people, but more important, it introduced to America all the most exciting new European literature of the time. Pirandello's *Six Characters in Search of an Author,* Gertrude Stein's plays, Max Jacob's prose poems—there was very little Loeb and his editors missed. When it came to American poetry, their taste was somewhat more conventional, but then so too were American poets. The avantgarde poets of the day, all of them published in *Broom,* were Hart Crane, Raymond E. F. Larsson, Malcolm Cowley, and Yvor Winters, and I suppose as a group they were thought of by younger people as marking a turning point, a watershed in American poetry not unlike Apollinaire in French.

Hart Crane was really a junior product of *The Seven Arts* group, an inheritor of the Whitman mystique. He fancied himself an avatar of Poe, Whitman, Rimbaud, and Christopher Marlowe, and he really was like all of them rolled into one. His verse owes much to the primitive dramatic iambic pentameter of Marlowe and Thomas Kyd and to their Euphuism, their flamboyant, manneristic, distortion of language. He is the last person to attempt to reproduce Whitman's epic of The American Dream, and he came to think of his attempt, *The Bridge,* as a failure, both on his part and on America's. He was more alienated than Poe and as haunted, and like Rimbaud, he sought passionately a willed derangement of the sensibility, and ecstasy in the literal sense, a standing outside oneself. "*Je suis un autre.*" Of all the translations of Rimbaud that have been made,

91

Hart Crane's *Voyages* are by far the most Rimbaudian, and they are not translations at all, but imitations. Hart Crane never managed more than a meager conversational knowledge of the French language. In the years since, Crane's reputation has gone up and down, but he has always been read, and has influenced writers as diverse as the Welsh Dylan Thomas, the Scot, W. S. Graham, and Allen Ginsberg.

Yvor Winters is a very considerable poet indeed, with a most curious career. Out of all his generation he was the one who read the modern European poetry in the original languages and for pleasure, and furthermore with understanding and assimilation. Poets slightly younger than himself eagerly read everything he published, from the earliest poems by "Arthur Winters" or "A. Y. Winters" in *The Double Dealer* and *The Little Review* to his fully developed first style in *Broom,* and they looked on him as an explorer and leader for their generation.

Reading the Imagist Manifesto one might think that the resulting poetry would be something like Pierre Reverdy. With the Imagists it was not, but it was with Yvor Winters. He pushed the intense sensitivity of H.D. to the breaking point, and he did it with a more radically dissociated and reconstructed verse, with a new prosodic power, and with, to put it simply, more content. Winters' early poems are overtly erotic or philosophical; besides being more "abstract" (a foolish word to apply to the art of words) they are more concrete and communicative than those of any of his predecessors. He was incomparably the best poet to have developed in the post-war Chicago school centered in the University, which included Glenway Wescott, Elizabeth Madox Roberts, Mark Turbyfill, Samuel

Putnam, Maureen Smith, and Janet Lewis, later Mrs. Winters.

When most of his friends and most of his literary generation went to Paris and met the great, Winters discovered he had fairly advanced tuberculosis and was forced to live the rest of his life in a dry climate. He taught school for a while in an ugly mining town, Raton, New Mexico, and then college in Moscow, Idaho, and finally in the late Twenties he came to Stanford, where he remained for the rest of his life. He was the true exile, the true *aliené*. Years must have gone by where nobody knew what he was talking about except his wife, or his echoing students. He became cranky and cantankerous and is responsible for some of the most wrong-headed and eccentric criticism ever written.

He changed the style of his verse to a stark neo-classicism of his own invention, which he always insisted owed much to, of all people, the late Tudor writer of doggerel, Barnaby Googe. Actually he is more like Walter Savage Landor, whom he admired, or A. E. Housman, whom he did not. His great admiration was Paul Valéry, and his poems are somewhat like a highly simplified Paul Valéry, an eccentric divagation from Valéry. The unconscious motive was probably épatéism, *pour épater les avant-gardistes*. Winters' Barnaby Googe is to Eugene Jolas as Marcel Duchamp's urinal labelled "Mutt" is to George Babbitt. Winters stood Dadaism on its head, as Marx did Hegel, and his critical ideas cannot be appreciated unless this is understood. They were designed to give Eugene Jolas running and barking fits.

At Stanford Winters built a highly disciplined little school of poets in almost no time at all. They were taught to write according to specific rules and with a single strictness, far greater than anything in any neo-classic tradition, something perhaps like the *skalds* and *filidhs* in ancient Scandinavia and Ireland. It didn't seem to do them any harm. A generation later, after Winters was dead, they were still amongst some of the best poets around, notably J. B. Cunningham and Ann Stanford, and as a group there had never been anything like them in the history of American poetry.

Years later, past middle age, Winters tried to organize another circle, a second generation of his "poets of the Pacific." Some of them, Scott Momaday, Alan Stevens, Thom Gunn, Edgar Bowers, deserve to be better known. But none of these people made the impression the earlier group had. He is an example of what a great teacher, however wrong-headed, can do. After all, the first group were just people who liked to write poems who happened to be going to Stanford. Horace Gregory once called him, paraphrasing Hokusai, "an old man mad about poetry"—when he was still less than forty years old.

Malcolm Cowley, long ago, when he was still young, was called by Alfred Kreymborg a great disappointment, simply because he didn't write enough. In his youth Cowley seemed to combine in his poems the localism of William Carlos Williams, the American mystique of *The Seven Arts,* and the Alfred Stieglitz circles, and the influence of Amy Lowell, to whom in fact he submitted his poems for advice, and the Midwest Populists, all transferred to Cowley's own native locale, West Central Pennsylvania. When he eventually collected his poems in one volume he called the book *Blue Juniata,* after the beautiful river by which he grew up.

He went from Harvard to war, and after the war stayed on in Paris. He and his friend Matthew Josephson came to know the leaders of French Dadaism, Tzara, Aragon, Soupault, and the rest. At first they were associated with *Secession,* published in Europe, which spoke for an updating of *The Seven Arts* tradition. At the end of its career they took over *Broom* from Harold Loeb.

Now Yvor Winters with his Barnaby Googe was not alone in his Dadaism in reverse. The Dadaists before they turned into Surrealists did much the same thing. From anarchist revolutionaries giving expression to the broken heart of Europe, they suddenly became worshippers of all things American. They wrote novels in imitation of Nick Carter and made movies, they thought, in imitation of Charlie Chaplin, who became for them a demigod. They painted pictures of skyscrapers which they had never seen, and wrote poems in imitation of American advertising copy, and serious essays on the tragic art of the movie cowboy—William S. Hart. *Américanisme* became a craze of the international avant-garde, even of the Russian Comfuturists and Constructivists—at last even of the Americans. Gilbert Seldes wrote a book, *The Seven Lively Arts,* which proved conclusively that the forms of the mass culture were greatly superior to the fine arts of the elite. Bob Cody years before had run a magazine *Soil,* devoted to the same thesis. Here began that highbrow adoration of monstrous skyscrapers, B movies, and billboards which endures to this day. Cowley, Josephson, Robert Coates, Slater Brown, Bob Brown, and their friends became enthusiastic converts and turned *Broom* into an organ of a thoroughly Frenchified *américanisme* and brought the magazine back to America with plans to turn it into a popular publication competing with *Vanity Fair*. Alas! America did not recognize itself in this mirror and soon *Broom* ceased publication.

In the meantime Cowley had written some very amusing and rambunctious poems, the only surviving examples of *américanisme* except for Robert Coates' novel *Eater of Darkness* and some of the short stories in Kenneth Burke's *White Oxen*. Matthew Josephson published a book of similar poems but almost all the copies were destroyed in a fire. Although associated with them, e. e. cummings did not really write in this style. His poetry is a perfectly natural expression of the mass culture.

Josephson went into business for a while, became an editor of the small publishing house, Macauley, and published lots of his friends' books, and then became a professional biographer. For many years Cowley was literary editor of *The New Republic* and wrote little poetry. When the Italian immigrant anarchists Sacco and Vanzetti were executed hundreds of poems in memory and in protest were written, and the best of them all was Cowley's "For St. Bartholomew's Eve." Then for years he was ignored as a poet, to be rediscovered only recently.

Two other poets who dropped out of sight were Raymond Larsson, the best Catholic poet of his time and the best of the early followers of T. S. Eliot, and Jean Toomer, who really belongs with *The Seven Arts* group and whose work much resembles that of the novelist Waldo Frank. Larsson became ill and spent over thirty years in the hospital.

Toomer turned to mystical religion and denounced poetry and renounced race—he was certainly the best American Negro poet until the upsurge of creativity amongst Blacks after 1960. He refused to allow his poetry to be reprinted or anthologized, and as he was dying turned over his literary estate to his friend Arna Bontemps, and his one book of poems and stories, *Cane,* was republished with great success. Larsson unfortunately has not been rediscovered, though he is remembered with respect and affection by his contemporaries.

This time, the years of Coolidge prosperity, was also the period of The Harlem Renaissance. The days, as Langston Hughes says in a bitter chapter heading of his autobiography, "When the Negro Was in Vogue," and it was fashionable for the beautiful people to go up to Harlem seeking Dark Gods at The Cotton Club where they would sway and jerk to the melancholy music of the imperturbable Duke Ellington as though it was savage jungle rhythms designed to accompany a supper of missionary soup. No literary cocktail party on Park Avenue was complete without the presence of the blond Nordic Negrophile Carl Van Vechten. All the highly civilized great rich competed furiously for the chance to patronize a Negro poet.

And then came 1929, the stock market crash, and the World Economic Crisis. The Harlem Renaissance turned out to have been a fad of white New York, and the bottom fell out of it. Most of the poets dropped from sight. Only the hardiest survived and most of them found an audience only in what then, in the Thirties, was the New Left. Actually it was only in the Left, in the old *Masses, Mother Earth,* the *Liberator,* and the monthly *New Masses,* and in the social world of revolutionary bohemia, Communist and anarchist, that Negroes ever had been treated as equals and judged on their own merits. (There was considerable covert racism in the Socialist Party and the IWW.) Whatever their personal opinions, Claude MacKay, Countee Cullen, Fenton Johnson, Langston Hughes, Arna Bontemps, even

Jean Toomer when young, were perforce men of the Left. Their Negro audience was infinitesimal and the only white people who really wanted to associate with them or read them were Socialists, Communists, and anarchists. This is still true. The present-day fad for Black is Beautiful amongst students and intellectuals of the white upper middle class is only slightly less superficial than the craze of the jazz age, when the Negro was in vogue, and may vanish as quickly. There were mini-skirts in the spring of 1929, too. Then the economy collapsed and there were maxi-skirts again. By and large the Negro writer in America has been at home only amongst the alienated, for the simple reason that he, as LeRoi Jones has said, is alienated on inspection. The Negro has nowhere else to turn. His only enduring sources are in his folk culture, and the literary *assimilado* has never been able to compete successfully except on the level of the mass culture—Frank Yerby or E. Sims Campbell or before them the Shakespearean actor Ira Aldridge, and the painter Henry O. Tanner. Three of these people as soon as they could went to Europe and stayed there.

VIII.

WHEN *Broom* died, its place was taken by Eugene Jolas's *transition,* which closed out the Lost Generation, saw at last the expatriates go home, and ran well into the years of the World Economic Crisis. Those were the years when Surrealism was in flower and Jolas's special personal variation of that movement gave the magazine a certain arrogance—of point of view, but not of contents. If anything, *transition* was more catholic than *Broom.* It was also better informed about European literature generally and printed the prose poems of Novalis alongside those of Hans Arp, hands joined in willed hallucination across a century.

Jolas was of Lorrainer parentage and was discovered working as a newspaperman in New Orleans by Sherwood Anderson and was introduced to the editors of *The Double Dealer.* He published a book of poems with an introduction by Anderson, married, and went to Paris where, with guile and luck, he always managed to find money to finance his magazine, the most influential, if not the best, in any language, of the period. He spoke English, French, and German equally well and seems to have had at least a reading knowledge of Dutch and Italian.

The Italian Futurist Marinetti had taught the avant-garde to look on anything written before themselves as *passéist,* and Greek Surrealists in Paris dismissed Homer as just a long-dead versifying Venizelos or Metaxas. Jolas was far from being a time-bound provincial. He was above all other things interested in building permanent foundations for the post-modern sensibility and he ransacked time and space for his material. Novalis, Jacob Boehme, Hölderlin, the spiritual alchemist Thomas Vaughan, the *I Ching,* A. E. Waite, Nicholas Flammel, John of the Cross, Anglo-Saxon spells, American Indian songs, African witch doctors' incantations, St. Pol Roux's visions and Raphael Alberti's angels, Jolas read them all, usually before anybody else, including Breton, in the Surrealist movement, discussed them excitedly with his friends, and printed as many examples of Dionysiac visionary art from all the ends of the earth as he could.

As long as it lasted *transition* ran in almost every issue an installment of James Joyce's *Finnegans Wake,* then called *Work in Progress.* Unfortunately Jolas was converted by Joyce's orgy of neologisms and came to believe in what he called The Revolution of the Word as in a new religion. He actually thought that it would be possible not just to revolutionize the syntax of language, to break up and recombine words themselves, using not only English words but words from other languages as well, until one had evolved and mastered an international Surrealist Esperanto whose syntax would be the subconscious associationism of dream and echolalia, a direct reflection of the real structure of reality. This is an impressive theory, and it's a pity that it didn't work. A few of Jolas's friends tried to write that way but managed to produce only ephemeral literary curiosities.

The first number of *transition* featured poems by the French Surrealist Robert Desnos which he said were produced in the free association of trance states. Actually one of them, his best known poem until he came to rewrite it and improve it on his death bed, is a paraphrase of a poem by the sixteenth-century French poet, Maurice Scève. Desnos was a great put-on artist and the first "post-modern" intellectual in 1925. In 1970 there would be, conservatively estimated, a million or more Desnoses running around over the earth. Jolas was smart enough to accept Desnos as mentor, and from him learned of Tarot cards as a method of composition, hallucinogenic mushrooms as a means, the total subversion of the reason and sensibility of the Established Mind, the Social Lie, as an end—along with an appreciation of jazz (Desnos ran a radio jazz program). He was discovered alive in a stack of corpses in Terezina concentration camp in Czechoslovakia and died of the effects of starvation before he could be really restored to life—but he wrote the final version of the great Last Poem to Yuki, his girl. Desnos was what Cocteau pretended to be, and what Allen Ginsberg tries to be, and often succeeds.

In the course of its life *transition* printed every important European modernist poet with special emphasis on the Surrealists and their allies, and this program was backed up with tireless exhortation and propaganda for the revolution of the world. Very few American poets did not read *transition,* yet all this explosion had little effect. The American poetry in the magazine went its way regardless. Favorites of Jolas, Bravig Imbs and Richard Thoma, for instance, were not very good. There were a few people with strange names, as though they had been born in the land of Esperanto—who turned out to be Jolas himself. Otherwise he relied on already well-known people like Raymond Larsson, Laura Riding, and Archibald MacLeish. The one person who came nearest to fulfilling the program developed in the pages of *transition* was Walter Lowenfels. But Lowenfels was not a free associationist, a dream poet like the Surrealists. Neither was he a revolutionist of the word inventing his own vocabulary. His poetry follows a method of dissociation and recombination of fairly large syntactic elements midway between *The Waste Land,* and the *Cantos,* and Apollinaire's *Zone,* and his sensibility, the feeling of his poetry, is remarkably like Apollinaire. He was over the heads of his own associates in Paris in those days, as can be seen by reading Henry Miller's satirical portrait of him, "Jabberwohl Kronstadt." He isn't really at all difficult to understand now that forty years have made us familiar with the idiom. His *Some Deaths,* on Hart Crane, Apollinaire, D. H. Lawrence, Rimbaud, taken together, make up one of the most successful of what his generation called "philosophical epics."

At the time Lowenfels, who was certainly not a member of any Lost Generation, nevertheless did think of himself as an expatriate—he had come to Paris to stay. As the world economy broke down and Fascism threatened France, he became increasingly politicized and, eventually, out of a sense of duty, returned to America, entered Left politics, and ceased to write verse for many years. He was indicted under the Smith Act as a Communist and started to write again while waiting trial. As time went on he became extremely popular with young people and one of the leaders of the revival of oral poetry in the Fifties and Sixties. He is the only person of his background who has managed to bridge the generation gap.

Robert McAlmon was one of the central figures of Paris-America. He started out as perhaps the best of the ultimate generation of Populist poets. He was also a short-story writer, novelist, and critic of outstanding ability. His poetry is not like anybody else's of his type. It is far more narrative and dramatic than Evelyn Scott's or Lola Ridge's and it is far more direct and far less sentimental. He married an English poetess of immense wealth, came to Paris, and with a tiny fraction of her family's money ran one of the most significant publishing enterprises of the time—*Contact* magazine, and Contact Editions, co-edited with William Carlos Williams. The *Contact Anthology* of his favorites among the writers he published included Djuna Barnes, Bryher, Mary Butts, Norman Douglas, Havelock Ellis, F. M. Ford, Wallace Gould, Ernest Hemingway, Marsden Hartley, H. D., John Herrman, James Joyce, Mina Loy, Robert McAlmon, Ezra Pound, Dorothy Richardson, May Sinclair, Edith Sitwell, Gertrude Stein, W. C. Williams. He is the amusing character who accompanies the hero in *The Sun Also Rises* on the fishing trip in the Pyrenées, the best writing Hemingway ever did, and McAlmon always claimed he had gone over that section with Hemingway and "polished" it. His autobiography, *Being Geniuses Together,* is a most perceptive record of *cette belle époque.* It has recently been reissued, edited and altered by Kay Boyle and interspersed with her own memories. The original edition is to be preferred.

Most of McAlmon's English and American contemporaries whom he published looked on him simply as a money tree, and paid little attention to his writing, but he was the only man amongst them who was understood, accepted, and assimilated by the French. It would be hard to find anybody less like the French poets and novelists of the late Dada and early Surrealist periods, but it was people like Philippe Soupault, Louis Aragon, Blaise Cendrars, who understood him best in those days, who welcomed him as an equal and remembered him with fondness, precisely because he was, like Gertrude Stein and William Carlos Williams, a bonafide American autochthone. He was also a friend of Ilya Ehrenberg's, who introduced him to the Russian literary public where he found widespread critical acceptance, because he fulfilled their idea of a Social Realist poet, something they themselves never managed to produce. On the other hand, there was only one book of his ever published by an American publisher, his selected poems, *Not Alone Lost,* which sold fewer copies than any other in the history of New Directions. A comparison of McAlmon's narrative poems with the self-conscious farmer poetry of Robert Frost or the cowgirl tragedies of Robinson Jeffers is an elementary lesson in literary discrimination. He, like Laura Riding, is a great lost poet.

McAlmon's most loyal surviving friend has been Kay Boyle. Her fiction and poetry might be called a lusher, more emotional, Irish version of McAlmon, who once called her the female Don Byrne. This does not mean it is bad; quite the contrary. McAlmon always kept his distance from his creations, like Stendhal. Kay Boyle is far more involved both with hers and with herself. It is significant that almost all of her poems carry dedications to specific people. She, like Walter Lowenfels, has managed to speak out of her generation across the notorious "gap" to the alienated youth of today. At the same time she has remained passionately loyal to her companions of her own youth, to McAlmon, Carnevali, Lowenfels, Nancy Cunard, Aragon, Soupault, and to Ernest Walsh, another forgotten man. Kay Boyle is outstanding amongst successful writers of her period in being a person of unwavering principle and faithfulness.

Ernest Walsh edited for a very brief period one of the most exciting of the "expatriate" magazines, *This Quarter.* He died very young of tuberculosis and left behind a few poems somewhat like Kay Boyle's, but in my opinion weakened by sentimentality. The magazine, however, had it only managed a few more issues, would have been as epochal as *Broom, transition*, or *Contact*.

Nobody had more flair or more money to spend on publishing than Harry and Caresse Crosby. Crosby was the nephew of J. P. Morgan and Caresse the former wife of a Morgan partner. Harry was a violently explosive poet who wrote one beautiful book of erotic prose poems, *Sleeping Together*, something like Yvan and Claire Goll's *Dix mille aubes*, and toward the end of his life a series of hallucinated poems something like the last poems of Antonin Artaud's, except that Crosby's madness was the belief that he was the sun, or sometimes the bride of the sun. Caresse won the *parade aux poils* of the models at the *Quatre Arts* ball three times running until they discovered that she was not a *oiseau montparnassienne*, but an American millionairess, and disqualified her. Their Black Sun Press published all sorts of people—James Joyce, D. H. Lawrence—and, in the first paperback pocket books, alas a generation too soon, McAlmon's *Indefinite Huntress*, a superlative collection of short stories. After Harry's suicide, Caresse continued to publish, and after the Second War, her *Portfolio* introduced a second post-war generation of artists and writers to the world. She went around Europe on the heels of the Allied armies, before the bridges were back up and the through trains running, discovering painters and poets in the ruins.

There were other publishers—Shakespeare and Company (Sylvia Beach), Adrienne Monnier, the Three Mountains Press, Nancy Cunard's Hours Press, the second *This Quarter*, edited by Edward Titus, the husband of Helena Rubinstein, the magazine *Tambour*, edited by Harold Salemson, a very young American who had the honor of printing the first manifesto demanding a Popular Front after the Stavisky riots threatened France with Fascism. Sam Putnam came from Chicago and published for a while the *New Review*. Most of these people wrote memoirs, and reading them all is an enthralling experience. It is easy to believe that this was the high point, not just of Western European civilization, arts, and letters, but of vital human relationships as well.

After *transition* had been going a little while, a precocious young Southerner, Charles Henri Ford, founded the little magazine *Blues* and later took Parker Tyler on as co-editor. *Blues* was more open to radical young avantgardists than was *transition*. Interestingly enough, very few of them were living in Paris, but were scattered all over America. The number of people Ford and Tyler discovered or published when they were still practically unknown is astonishing. They discovered Erskine Caldwell, Edouard Roditi, and me in one issue. Later during the Second World War they became avowed Surrealists and again discovered a whole gallery of American Surrealist poets and painters. They themselves and their young associate editor of *View*, Philip Lamantia, are in fact practically the only successful American Surrealists, until recently.

Ford and Tyler may have been Southerners, but they were hardly typical. From the early Twenties, based on Vanderbilt University, a deliberate, highly self-conscious, tightly organized, reactionary movement was under way. This was the Fugitives group, named after their magazine, *The Fugitive*. The title was chosen to indicate that they were fugitives from every aspect of modernity, philosophical, social, literary, political. They were militant defenders of the Myth of the Old South, long since debunked by Mark Twain as a pipe dream resulting from falling asleep

106

over the novels of Sir Walter Scott. They read T. S. Eliot's *Criterion* and Maurras' *L'Action Française* and tried to put their principles into practice amongst the corn and cotton. They allied themselves with the briefly notorious "Humanist Movement" and came to call themselves Southern Agrarians—by which they meant an amateurish concoction of the Girondins, the Physiocrats, Thomas Jefferson, that pretended to represent the aristocratic values of a yeoman-based, Southern high culture. Their ideologue was not John Crowe Ransom (he was their overseer) but a poetaster and professor named Donald Davison whose social tracts greatly resemble speeches given by Senator Bilbo, or a generation later, Senator Eastland, to the Annual Convention of the Mississippi Browning Society. Their literary principles were equally reactionary. At first they imitated the Baroque poets of the Elizabethan and Jacobean period, the so-called "metaphysicals" whom Eliot had made fashionable, and then they were introduced by their most incongruous member to the broken rhythms of the Chaucerian decadence—Occleve and Lydgate, the deliberate doggerel of Skelton and to the rugged, consciously distorted rhythms of Donne's *Satyres* and the plays of John Marston.

This incongruous member was Laura Riding, by far the best poet of the group, and the only woman. She was not a Southerner but was at that time at the University of Illinois. She was the only member who was Jewish, otherwise the Fugitives were pure Aryans. More of Laura Riding in a moment.

As the economic crisis deepened, American society became as highly polarized as German or French, and almost all writers to greater or lesser degree moved to the Left. There had to be some writers around the Right pole, but America, where everybody is liberal and progressive, was very short of Right writers. The Southern Agrarians were only too happy to meet the need, to fill the vacuum in the American *Geist*. They already occupied certain strategic positions and they were as highly organized as the Left. It is hard to realize today when "everybody teaches" that they were the only group in America entirely based upon the universities. All of them already were academicians. They had in the days of "Humanist controversy" staked out a number of influential book-reviewing claims. (It should be explained that "Humanism" was a drive on the part of conservative and academic critics under the leadership of Irving Babbitt, teacher of French at Harvard and disciple of Maurras, to capture book-reviewing jobs from the followers of H. L. Mencken and the Midwesterners.) From then on they drove steadily toward a takeover of contemporary writing, editing, publishing, and teaching. They did not succeed, but they were unaware of it. As the years went by they formed an alliance with the ex-Communist militant anti-Stalinists and to this day this outlandish United Front believes it is all the contemporary literature there is. Their best poets were their oldest member, John Crowe Ransom, their ambassador to bohemia, Allen Tate, and their precocious junior mascot, Robert Penn Warren—always excepting Laura Riding. It is interesting that this group, who with all-inclusive historical generosity called themselves the Reactionary Generation, never managed to produce as many good truly conservative and traditional poets as Yvor Winters did in his first two years on the Stanford campus.

Except Laura Riding. Laura Riding is the greatest lost poet in American literature. W. H. Auden once called her the only living philosophical poet. Even when she was Laura Riding Gottschalk, a young "faculty wife" in the inhospitable environment of Champaign, Illinois, her first book, *The*

Closed Chaplet, contained poems quite unlike anyone else's —a little like some of the more gruesome folk poetry of the French *Mère d'oie*—witty, deceptively simple, and prosodically eccentric. Although it was she, and not Ransom, who was responsible for the revival of John Skelton, her poems that look like Skelton's are characterized by a rhythm all her own. Prosody is to poetic rhythm as written music is to jazz. The discoveries of Laura Riding's subtle ear escape analysis.

Toward the end of the decade, she left America, first for England where she became the living archetype of Robert Graves' *White Goddess,* and the teacher of a whole group of poets, Auden and his circle at Oxford, William Empson and his circle at Cambridge, and in an older generation, the philosopher-critic I. A. Richards, and Robert Graves himself. She seems to have baffled T. S. Eliot and kept him off balance all during her stay in England. She had a similar effect on the Sitwells who made waspish remarks about her. Wyndham Lewis, as obstreperous as she, was a devoted admirer.

She was closely associated with Robert Graves all during her years abroad, first in London and then in Majorca where together they ran the Seizin Press and published the magazine *Epilogue.* She turned Graves around in midcareer and made an entirely different poet and personality of him. His theories of matriarchy, the rugged metric and dry wit of his later poetry, and his position as an outsider to the modernist establishment developed during his companionship with Laura Riding. They seemed to have worked together perfectly and took up one interest or enthusiasm or intellectual position after another in perfect unanimity. They wrote quite a bit of fiction about historical figures of Greece and Rome, like two new and bitter Plutarchs. Laura

109

Riding's excellent stories and novels have been forgotten. Robert Graves' *I Claudius* and *Claudius the God* were immensely popular and are still in print. They wrote a lot of very funny criticism in joint authorship, and their *Survey of Modernist Poetry* and *A Pamphlet Against Anthologies* are still wonderfully entertaining reading. Of course some of their judgments are wrong-headed, but so are those of all great critics.

Laura Riding's criticism published under her own name alone is amongst the best ever written by an American. Her *Jamais Plus, The Case of Monsieur Poö* settles hilariously *that* question once and for all. Her pieces on the esthetics of poetry, which were too abstruse for her time, are much more perceptive and far more profound than those of Eliot or Richards or Empson, but they are certainly deliberately written to be as unpopular as possible.

Committed by *A Pamphlet Against Anthologies*, she has never permitted herself to be anthologized after the first *Fugitives* collection or even to be quoted, and so she is almost unknown today—in a time and in a worldwide counter culture where she would be most welcome, understood, and appreciated. I have never read her to students or friends without eliciting the most excited, enthusiastic response. Yet I might well get a letter threatening to sue me for admitting to reading her in the classroom. For many years she has lived out of the literary world altogether, in a small town in Florida, where, the last I knew, she was writing a dictionary as revolutionary as her poetry. There's never been anybody else quite like her. Nearest comes Wyndham Lewis, that other great outsider, who greatly admired her and printed her in his magazine, *The Enemy*, and she and Graves reciprocated in their *Epilogue*. She would certainly be popular amongst the new feminists, for, to quote from a writer in a little magazine of the time, "It is rumored that Laura Riding, over her bed in a half-ruined castle by the sea, outside Palma in Majorca, has written in letters of gold, GOD IS A WOMAN."

I cannot make this personal tribute too fulsome. Laura Riding has meant more to me than any other American poet, and in the years since her retirement she has been a woman much missed. I think the history of the last thirty years of American poetry would have been different had she been around.

Louis Zukofsky, whose "Poem Beginning The" was a discovery of Ezra Pound's in his magazine *Exile* and created a small sensation, tried to start an organized movement of the European type. He published an Objectivists' number of *Poetry Magazine,* a complicated manifesto essay on Objectivism, and an *Objectivists' Anthology,* and then went on in partnership with George Oppen, with a small press, "To, Publishers." Almost all the people that Zukofsky picked as Objectivists didn't agree with him, didn't write like him or like one another, and didn't want to be called Objectivists. However, his own poetry, Carl Rakosi's, George Oppen's, and Charles Reznikoff's "found poems," do together constitute a definite school, based largely on the simple esthetics of William Carlos Williams' "no ideas but in things."

Eli Siegal was another independent, with somewhat similar theories which he called "aesthetic realism"—of poetry. He is still writing, still unjustly ignored, or put down as "just a Greenwich Village poet," still one of the most original, and perhaps the wittiest, poets of his time. Louis Grudin, now forgotten, was another.

For almost twenty years while the Proletarians and the Reactionaries ruled the roost, they were ignored not-people,

111

and, for sure, not-poets. They were not forgotten, however, by Patchen, myself, and a few others, and came to have a great influence on Charles Olson, Robert Creeley, and the Black Mountain school of the Fifties. Most of them have been published and republished in recent years and have found enthusiastic readers. Some of them have even been awarded prizes—but not by the literary Establishment that has survived from the last decade between the wars. They are now amongst the very small number of influential and respected poets from their generation. They are not only amongst the best, but they are amongst the most readable. On the other hand, it is hard indeed for you to get through the poetry of William Empson or John Crowe Ransom if you are an American poet born after 1935.

IX.

It is an article of faith with Marxists that economic, social, and political developments precede literary, but the evidence of history is all to the contrary. The rationalistic, intensely secular poetry of John Dryden written to a Protestant despot and a Catholic king anticipate the age of Reason, inaugurated by William of Orange and the Great Revolution, about whom he refused to write at all. The proletarian poetry of the Red Thirties was anticipated by two of the best poets of that school, Kenneth Fearing and Horace Gregory, both of whom published in *Blues*. Both came out of the Midwest. Both were conscious of fulfilling the unfulfilled promise of Carl Sandburg, each in a different way. Gregory's earliest poems take off from Sandburg's great portraits, "Dynamiter," "Chick Lorimer," and the rest, but they are more extended, more detailed, and more dramatic, and in this resemble some of the epitaphs in Masters' *Spoon River Anthology* and Sherwood Anderson's portraits in *Winesburg, Ohio* and *The Triumph of the Egg*. Unlike so much verse about the working class they show an ability to identify with real men and women rather than man in the abstract. In a period when, both Right and Left, impersonality was considered a leading virtue in poetry, Gregory's poems, whether about himself or others, are intensely personal, and many of them are in direct speech. No other poet in those days used the first- and second-person singular pronouns more naturally and unself-consciously than Gregory. For many years his most popular book has been his translation of Catullus, still the best ever done by an American. His verse is very definitely his own. His attitudes, his rhythms, the unanalyzable thing called style, have something elegiac and Latinate about them, although not at all obvious except to one familiar with the hard, acidulous, slightly weary poetry of Martial, Juvenal, and Petronius or the satirical poetry of Catullus.

Perhaps it is this foreignness—Horace Gregory bears a certain resemblance to an eighteenth-century Latinate Irish gentleman of letters—which has kept him from the appreciation he deserves. Then too like everybody who was early on the Left, the latecomers pretended he had never been, and to the Reactionaries "he didn't write poetry at all," as Robert Lowell once said of him at the poetry gathering at Bard College immortalized in Mary McCarthy's *Groves of Academe,* lumping him with non-poets like Sandburg, Oppenheim, Lola Ridge, and Whitman

Superficially much alike in their early years, Kenneth Fearing is really a very different kind of poet from Horace Gregory. If he takes off from Sandburg he takes off from tirades like "To a Contemporary Bunk Shooter." His poetry is rhetorical, denunciatory, agitational in intent, and his satires are directed not at people, but archtypes, stereotypes out of the *commedia dell'arte* of Middle America. He is the Juvenal of the Swing Vote. But also no other American poet of his time so closely identified himself with the working class, with the *lumpen* proletariat, with the impoverished stratum of the underworld, with hustlers, grifters, "nifties, yeggs, and thirsties," and no one else so completely immersed himself in the lingo of the mass culture.

Matthew Josephson might write an intellectual article all about how a piece of advertising copy was great art because he had written that particular piece of advertising copy himself. Kenneth Fearing didn't think like an advertising copywriter. He thought like the advertising copy itself, or at least like a taxi driver reading a billboard while fighting traffic. His contemporaries called him "the leader of the taxi-driver school of verse." There's a wonderful portrait of him in Albert Harper's *Union Square,* talking in a Brooklyn cab-driver accent in a conversation made up almost exclusively of advertising slogans. *"I'm not rich, I'm not poor; I just go along living quietly with my small circle of friends. Buy Buick!"* There's a lot more to Kenneth Fearing than collages of the unconscious practical jokes of the mass culture. He was the first eschatological American poet. For him apocalypse had already come and his poems are about the Seven Last Things—Death, Purgatory, Heaven, Hell, the Fire and the Judgment, but no Resurrection. For the Proletarian poets who flourished during the Thirties, the revolution was just around the corner. For Kenneth Fearing Western Civilization was already dead on its feet, a walking corpse bled of all value.

There are a number of American poets between the wars who were independent of all groups, tendencies, fashions, and other literary contacts. The most conspicuous was Robinson Jeffers. He started out a very conventional, sentimental poet with two privately printed books of the sort that constantly appear in provincial America. In 1925 *Tamar and Other Poems,* also privately printed, came out. He mailed it out to various well-known poets and critics. Its reception was sensational. From then on he published a series of books which were, for poetry in those days, bestsellers. Each one contained a highly melodramatic verse novel as well as shorter poems, all of them situated in the Big Sur Coast below Carmel, California, and in the Santa Lucia Mountains behind.

The novels have been called modern Greek tragedies and

his quantitative free verse, echoing the Greek hexameter, has been compared to Homer. Other critics, notably Yvor Winters in a conclusively devastating essay, have called his verse rhetorical and pretentious, free doggerel, his tragedies sensational melodrama, and his pessimistic philosophy sentimental. California embraced him enthusiastically. He certainly shares with Joaquin Miller and George Sterling the overwrought melodrama that seems to strike some ecological chord in the literary public of that melodramatic state, and his plots bear a distinct resemblance in tone and in underlying philosophy to the hard-boiled school of detective-story writers who flourished in Hollywood in his days—but without the irony of Dashiell Hammett, Raymond Chandler, or Horace McCoy. It is interesting to compare him to Ernest Haycox and Gordon Young, two writers who found material for stories resembling Joseph Conrad or the Greek tragedians in the thinly populated dramatic scenery of the far West. They are so even-handed, so objective and quiet in style, while Jeffers is always strained and rhetorical. The most illuminating comparison is between Jeffers' adaptation of Euripides' *Medea* and the original. In some of his shorter poems his *fin de siècle* pessimism is as convincing as John Davidson or Fitzgerald's *Rubaiyat*. But one is always reminded of Winters' remark that the statement, "It is better to be a rock than a man," is nonsense and therefore dishonest. However, the incidental local color and descriptions of nature repay the effort of reading the unconvincing melodramas, which is more than can be said for Joaquin Miller and George Sterling.

On the other side of the country John Wheelright, descended in all branches of his family tree from Boston Brahmins, and certainly in the thick of things, literary and political, in his day, was nonetheless, perhaps because of the sheer force of his personality, a singularly independent poet. He was more open to international influences and more engaged than most of his contemporaries. He was a Trotskyite, an Anglo-Catholic, and a most perceptive critic of architecture, and as poet, revolutionary, architect, and Catholic he was a totally committed activist. He was also one of the last of his kind in America, a great aristocratic eccentric. His poetry is full of hidden references and echoes. It does not need notes, but if anyone chose to annotate it, it would require far more apparatus per line than Eliot's or Pound's, but unlike theirs, this is not at all apparent. He was one of the best-read persons in every imaginable field that I have ever met, capable of carrying on a conversation about the snails of South America, the theoretical foundations of Russian anarchism, and the medieval English Rite of Sarum simultaneously. He was struck down late at night by a drunken driver on the bridge over the Charles River which his father had built, and died at the age of forty-three. His early death was an immeasurable loss to American poetry.

Three friends of Jack Wheelwright's, all classical scholars, form a little group by themselves—Dudley Fitts, Robert Fitzgerald, and Richmond Lattimore. They have made some of the finest translations from Greek and Latin ever done which have become standard to our time, but each in his own way is a poet of clarity, wit, and control, independent of movements and tendencies and literary cabals, and so not as appreciated as he should be.

We have now moved to a later literary generation, people born in the early years of the century who came to maturity in the troubled times after 1929. It was a lean season for American poetry. Hundreds of young intellectuals who started out as writers were consumed and cast aside by the Communist Party. Most of them became political activists and gave up writing. The strong-willed ones obeyed the

117

Party Line and dutifully wrote Proletarian literature and Socialist Realism. The stultifying effects of bureaucratic control are more than conclusively shown by the fact that all this passionate activity and commitment produced, in poetry, almost nothing of enduring value. America's revolutionary poets, Socialist and anarchist, flourished mostly in the old, free, Radical Movement before 1927, the year of Stalin's seizure of power, and those that came after belonged to dissident groups, mostly Trotskyites. Herman Spector, Sol Funaroff, Joseph Caylor, Edwin Rolfe, are probably the best out of hundreds. Kenneth Fearing was always independent and suspect, and Kenneth Patchen, the best of all the poets of the Left of those days, soon became so, and Patchen, of whom more later, is the only one who is still read.

It is hard for people to realize today, after a generation of enforced mediocrity and tendentiousness—"Socialist Realism"—that Russia, not France or Germany, was for a brief time the home of the most revolutionary departures in the arts. In painting, literature, and music, drama, dance, Russian developments in the first twenty years of the twentieth century were original and independent. Russian poets and artists were inspired by the examples of German Expressionism, French Cubism, and Italian Futurism, but actual influence from abroad was unimportant. Russian Futurism, for instance, was quite a different thing from the Italian, and the Russians probably first used the word.

By the outbreak of the First War Russian revolt in the arts had gone to more extreme lengths than anything in the West and the impulse toward completely non-objective painting, machine art, poetry of nonsense syllables, and an acrobatic theater was moving from East to West rather than the reverse. The first large-scale public exposure of the most avant-garde artists of the West itself was in designs for Diaghelieff's *Ballet Russe.*

Intellectual circles in Russia were far more radical in general social, political, and cultural matters than anywhere in the West since the 1840's in America. Free love, permissive education, birth control, vegetarianism, Tolstoyan pacifism, every variety of collective and individual anarchism, dress reform, total sexual equality, all sorts of crank medical theories—were commonplaces in not just advanced circles, but had ceased to shock cultivated people generally, while elsewhere in Europe the audience for Cezanne, Rimbaud, or Scriabin remained confined to small sectors of rebellious youth and the more decadent rich.

German Social Democracy, by contrast, no matter how Left, was hopelessly middle class in taste. Revolutionary art came to Germany from outcaste bohemians or from Russians like Kandinsky and El Lissitsky and Hungarians like Moholy-Nagy. During the severe famines of the Civil War period, the Bolsheviks sent hundreds of artists, writers, dance, theatre, and musical groups abroad, to earn hard currency and simply keep them from starving. Things Russian became a craze—especially Russian modernism—and the influence of people like Meierhold in the theatre and Eisenstein in the cinema and of the non-objective painters was vast and permanent, especially in America and Germany. Back in Russia, Maiakofsky, one of the greatest poets of the time in any language, and certainly one of the most "extreme," joined the Bolshevik Party. The abstract painters El Lissitsky and Wassily Kandinsky designed posters and a wide variety of visual education forms which were later to be absorbed by advertising and education in the West. The theater director Meierhold organized vast pageants. Constructivist artists-turned-architects designed creches and dairies, housing developments and monuments. Libertarian educational methods of the kind we identify with A. S. Neill and Paul Goodman were introduced into the regular school systems. All this had a tremendous influence abroad. The famous German Bauhaus was modelled on Russian examples which had never, due to the poverty of the Civil War period, come to fruition, and many of the Bauhaus artists, architects, and designers had worked in Russia shortly before or had been inspired by the Communist revolt in their own countries.

When French Cubism was a well-organized movement, almost all the Cubist painters were revolutionaries, Left Communists, or anarchists. The Dadaists of course were Nihilists properly so called, and from the beginning the Surrealists considered themselves Communists and were to break up when, as a group, they applied for membership in the Communist Party and were rejected unless they gave up their "petty bourgeois, formalist, social Fascist, decadent, degenerate," artistic methods.

All this was not without influence in the English-speaking world. The Scottish poet, Joseph Gordon McLeod, and the English poet and editor Edgell Rickword, are survivors from those days, and Edgell Rickword's magazine, the first to be called *The Left Review,* preceded the more famous Left poets of the later Thirties by several years. It is Edgell Rickword, along with Laura Riding, whose teaching is responsible for the modernist poetry of the young W. H. Auden, the best verse he ever wrote.

In America there were a number of little magazines which gave voice to this point of view. The most outstanding probably were *Left,* a handsome, well-illustrated, well-edited magazine, published by students at the University of Illinois, which was dedicated to a United Front of the already estranged revolutions in the arts and politics. Another was *Front,* USA editor Norman MacLeod, an indomitable editor of little magazines, a fair to medium poet, and a genuine internationalist. Macleod did an enormous, dedicated job of bringing together avant-garde writers all over America and cross-fertilizing them with European and Asian contacts. About this time the *Partisan Review,* the organ of the New York John Reed Club, the Communist artists' and writers' organization, revolted against the Party leadership (whose official cultural spokesman was the weekly *New Masses*), and committed itself to a similar policy.

The International Union of Revolutionary Artists and Writers called a world congress in Kharkov in the Ukraine. The spokesman of the modernists was the French Surrealist Louis Aragon. The Russian leadership demanded that they submit to discipline and become Social Realists or be expelled as Trotskyites. Aragon and some of his followers submitted. The majority of the Surrealists and other modern writers withdrew. One French delegate, René Crevel, killed himself when ordered to attack his former colleagues.

In a short time, back in America, the editors of the *Partisan Review* were expelled from the party for Trotskyite formalism, and the agitprop commission of the Communist Party ordered all writer members to "liquidate" all little magazines on which they had any influence, whether they were Communist in sympathy or not, and concentrate all effort and all money on the Sunday feature section of the *Daily Worker.* Needless to say, coming at the high point of the Red Thirties, these incredible decisions, ruthlessly applied to people who were not Party members at all, marked a climacteric in American—and worldwide—literary history. Letters were written to subscribers; angels were intimidated; editors were argued with in relays, and, if unconvinced, attacked and slandered. In one year dozens of little magazines went out of existence and hundreds of writers turned against at least the Stalinist form of Communism. None of them knew anything about Trotsky, but since they were accused of being Trotskyites, many decided to investigate. Few became members of the Left Opposition for any length of time, except in New York City. Many, like brides rejected at the church door, became embittered anti-Stalinists and eventually extreme reactionaries. The conspicuous tragedies were amongst the novelists, some of them the best and best-known of their day. Most of the poets, who had a much weaker grip on the public mind, simply vanished or became Party hacks.

Kenneth Patchen went his way regardless. He had not been an organization man when everybody else was, and he continued as an artistic and social revolutionary with only contempt for politics, revolutionary or counter-revolutionary. This earned him indifference or antagonism from his colleagues of a generation who preserved, through all changes of allegiance, the test charge, "You must be for us or against us; there is no middle ground." "No," said Patchen. "There isn't. But there is plenty of unoccupied ground on the deserted Left." For ten years Patchen was almost the only poet of the English language who remained a member of the international revolutionary literary avant-garde of better days. He may have been ignored by critics and editors but he was not ignored by the young. During the Second World War and the dark days of reaction afterwards he was the most popular poet on college campuses. He is still today an elder statesman of the youth revolt, the counter culture, and still today, he is never mentioned in the literary quarterlies.

Two other poets who began to publish in the years just before the Second War and who are still read today are Muriel Rukeyser and Richard Eberhart. Eberhart was associated with the group of "Metaphysicals" around William Empson at Cambridge and is still thought of by many people as an English poet. He is in fact by far the best of the Cambridge group with the possible exception of its youngest member, Kathleen Raine. Like her his poetry owes much to William Blake. Although he is in personal life conventional enough, with conventional attitudes, as a poet he seems to be, unbeknownst to himself, a mystic and religious pacifist-anarchist, and it was as such that he was welcomed by the poets of the post-war revolt in San Francisco, even though he went there as an officer in the Navy. Eberhart probably owes his wide acceptance by the post-war poets simply because he had never become part of the literary establishment of Southern Agrarians and disillusioned former members of the Left.

For a while between the wars "metaphysical" became a popular shibboleth of the poetry cliques. The term comes from the English (and Continental) baroque poets of intellectual wit of the late sixteenth and early seventeenth centuries—Marino, Góngora, Du Bartas, in Italy, Spain, and France, and a long line of Jacobean and Caroline poets in England, led in importance by John Donne, who was, deservedly, immensely popular in this period. Whatever they may have thought, William Empson, Louise Bogan, Leonie Adams, and the rest, did not write like John Donne, though Eberhart did, a little—but more, actually, like William Blake.

Muriel Rukeyser published her first poems while quite a young girl. While still in college she had already discovered her own special vocation, the poetic material, and the philosophical attitudes, which would endure throughout her work. Much of her early poetry was overtly social in its concerns, but it was far removed in style from the approved utterances of the Left, and even further removed in intent.

Her poems were the opposite of agitation and propaganda. They were expressions of responsibility, of abiding moral concern. As such they were part of a wider and more coherent life philosophy.

As time has gone on, her major poems have steadily increased in scope and depth and yet have at the same time become more intensely personal. Her great poem sequence, *Ajanta,* is not written as a piece of art criticism or travelogue. Like Pascal and his gulf, Muriel Rukeyser carries her Ajanta with her. If the social poems represent the fulfillment, in a more sophisticated age, of the Populist poets of the early years of the century, the later poems combine this concern with the enduring meanings of the feminine poets of those years raised to a new qualitative level. Like Eberhart and Patchen, Muriel Rukeyser was never assimilated by the Establishment. Perhaps it is her lack of frivolity which makes them angry. That and her total lack of provincialism. Few poets of her time have been more at home as internationalists and her translations of writers like Octavio Paz or Paul Éluard are distinguished by their capacity for natural, effortless, identification with their subjects.

Like Rukeyser, Eberhart, Merwin, John Ciardi is singularly independent, not just of the Establishment, but of literary movements and groups and tendencies. This gives his poetry a human, unliterary quality all too rare in his generation. I once said he looked more like a pilot for Alitalia than a poet, and that is what his poetry is like, the expression of the life and values of a well-educated, widely traveled, man of the world and as such has a far wider appeal than the work of over-specialized sensibilities. A popular lecturer, he has done much to educate the general public in the appreciation of poetry.

When we turn to the Establishment itself we find ourselves in an altogether smaller world. Delmore Schwartz, Elizabeth Bishop, Jean Garrigue, Robert Penn Warren— what characterizes these people is their narrowness, their lack of broad contact, or even interests, in anything but a narrow range of contemporary English and American poetry, Baroque English poetry, and their complication without complexity. Their intellectual horizons are strictly confined by the critical notions that descend from Charles Maurras, to Irving Babbitt, to T. S. Eliot, to I. A. Richards, thence to Cleanth Brooks, to Elizabeth Drewes, thence to a thousand or ten thousand classrooms. Their outstanding character is their strict avoidance of that virtue eminently shared by Patchen, Eberhart, and Rukeyser—responsibility. Reaction is always a fashion. Looking back over thirty years (at one's parents' generation) the old style is always revealed as crippled by frivolity and hypocrisy.

The war produced a tremendous explosion of poetry in beleaguered London and a revolution in poetic taste. In America, the war produced Karl Shapiro, Randall Jarrell, and Peter Viereck. Robert Lowell went to prison as a conscientious objector. It was a thin time for war poetry or anti-war poetry. The older poets were mostly chairborne, many of them in the OSS, the predecessor of the CIA. American poets, after a lifetime of opposition to war in any form, were embarrassed by the necessity to resist Hitler. Many took non-combatant jobs, but with the exception of Lowell, and to a lesser extent, Paul Goodman, few remained actual pacifists. Some, like Patchen, Theodore Roethke, John Berryman, Delmore Schwartz, were not subject to the draft. Others of the "younger poets" of those days were in fact too old, like Oscar Williams, Stanley Burnshaw, Stanley Kunitz, myself.

Listing these people, it is obvious, to anyone familiar with their work, what was happening. Poetry was loosening

125

up, becoming more directly communicative and personal, escaping from the influence of T. S. Eliot and the Reactionary Generation and the tight, overwrought style that imitated the English Baroque. Empson's "seven types of ambiguity" were suddenly at a discount. At the same time, the younger poets who were widely published and accepted during the war had become more conventional than their elders. The literary quarterlies were committed to the thesis that "the generation of experiment and revolt is over." Nothing could be less true. It is characteristic of cliques to think that they are all there is. Behind the scenes still younger people, and the ignored survivors of the generation of experiment and revolt, were preparing a complete *bouleversement*.

For over a generation modern literature has owed more to James Laughlin, publisher of New Directions, than to any other single person. All through the years when the avant-garde was not supposed to exist, he went bravely on, publishing them—everybody—from all languages—for many years at considerable financial loss. This is the kind of patronage that counts. It meant nothing for Otto Kahn to give Hart Crane a check for $1000. Laughlin worked day after day, often till far into the night, himself, and hard, to publish writers who often were far less good than himself, year after year, for little thanks. He is an excellent and original poet, and might have been writing his own poems. If he lived in a civilized country his chest would be covered with medals and his wall with honorary doctorates.

X.

THERE were three important centers of change during the Second War. European exiles, mostly French and mostly in New York, who resurrected Surrealism amongst American poets, the English New Romantics and Apocalyptics, poets like Dylan Thomas, David Gascoigne, George Barker, Henry Treece, W. S. Graham, who rejected what they called the social and classical idiom of W. H. Auden and C. Day Lewis (they claimed to have converted Stephen Spender) and the older objectivism of T. E. Hulme and T. S. Eliot, for a new intense personalism and a more discursive verse. Their principal spokesman in America was Oscar Williams, who in the Twenties had edited with his wife, Gene Derwood, a very personal and romantic magazine, *Rhythmus,* and who now, in a series of anthologies, introduced neo-Romantic taste to America.

The other focus of change was in San Francisco where there had grown up a resident emigration from the prevailing literary Establishment. As the war went on poetry from the underground publications of the French resistance began to reach America, especially San Francisco, along with the British magazines—Cyril Connelly's *Horizon,* Tambimuttu's *Poetry London,* Charles Wrey Gardiner's *Poetry Quarterly,* Alex Comfort's *Poetry Folios,* and George Woodcock's *Now,* the latter two avowedly anarchist-pacifist in emphasis. And after the war a number of people who had been in the occupation forces in Japan returned to America deeply influenced by Japanese culture. Charles Henri Ford and Parker Tyler, with Philip Lamantia, a young poet from San Francisco, edited the magazine *View* which was more than a revival of *Blues* or *transition*. It was, for its lifetime, the principal organ of Surrealism in exile, and as such, the expression of the third period of Surrealism, a different thing in many ways from the original united movement of the early Twenties, or the survivors of the Kharkov conference, who refused to accept the order to turn themselves into Socialist Realists. There were other magazines, notably Claire and Yvan Goll's *Hemispheres,* David Hare's *VVV,* whose editorial advisors were André Breton, Max Ernst, and Marcel Duchamp, and from Mexico, *DYN,* edited by the painter Wolfgang Paalen and his friends, which printed a number of new modernist American poets. Soon indigenous magazines of a new apocalyptic vision were springing up in America, led by George Leite's *Circle* in Berkeley, California, and *Ark,* the publication of the San Francisco Anarchist Circle, the first to state, in polemic, ideological terms, the call for a new revolutionary avant-garde. Just as in the First War, so in the Second, an historical epoch came to an end, and with it an entire culture complex, world-view, and even life style. Under the impact of a new technology the economy changed drastically from the old industrial financial pattern to the electronic, computerized, automated industries of the later half of the century. Keynesian economy became universal, however disguised. Hard work and careful saving became vices instead of virtues. Populations, even in the Communist countries, became ceaselessly mobile, both geographically

128

and up and down the social ladder. Old-fashioned imperial-ism became unprofitable and the former colonies of the dominant nations were "freed." Interpersonal relations underwent ever accelerating revolutionary changes. In Europe and North America the affluent society with its endless flow of commodities and steadily inflating money got under way. Television began its attrition of written literature which had lasted for five thousand years, an attrition whose end is not yet in sight.

The old political objectives and the alliances necessary to achieve them became meaningless—popular fronts, dictatorships of the proletariat, and corporative states went out of date along with Socialist Realism, Southern Agrarianism, "Royalism, Anglo-Catholicism, and Classicism." At the growing edge of world literature, the literary representatives of interbellum culture ceased to have meaning to the young and the post-modern culture. They were taken over by the academies. The most extreme radical and alienated writers and artists of the former generation became world influences, Antonin Artaud or Samuel Beckett replaced T. S. Eliot or André Gide. American Abstract Expressionism and the mystical ideographic painting of Morris Graves and Mark Tobey replaced the classicist-modernist and the social painters of America, and soon became popular all over the world.

W. H. Auden, Stephen Spender, C. Day Lewis, and their friends were dismissed as the "stately-home-weekend-soviets school of poetry" and Dylan Thomas, whose work seemed to oppose theirs at every point, became the first poet of worldwide mass popularity of the kind to become characteristic of the later years of the century. It is highly significant that this popularity was due to his readings, not to his books. For one person who bought and read Dylan Thomas in print, literally thousands crowded university auditoriums to hear him read.

The new affluence, the population explosion, the revolution of rising expectations, all led to an educational explosion, and within it an accelerated demand for education in the humanities, in the creative use of a new leisure. Within a very short time after the Second War, all but a few American poets of any reputation had been recruited into the universities. Every college in the land competed with every other to catch a "poet in residence." The old Establishment went straight from swivel chairs in Washington to classroom podiums in the most prestigious schools. Anyone who did not was looked on by his colleagues as a weird eccentric.

It began to seem that American literature would become completely Byzantinized, and even the most obstreperous *revoltés,* alcoholics, and deviants would be absorbed in an all-encompassing bureaucracy. This as a matter of fact has always been the condition of German literature and of Italian. Goethe was not an exception; he was the archetype. Even today the writers of Gruppe 47, set up under American auspices after the war, but dedicated to revolutionizing the German sensibility, have been from the inception of the group not *alienés* like Baudelaire, Flaubert, or André Breton, but part of the ruling structure of the society, each with his well-defined position on the ladder. Today this condition in America is an accomplished fact. There is a whole world of such people, and amongst them an immense cadre of writers, especially poets. But America is a more unruly country than most any other, a kind of rich, sanitary, educated Afghanistan. Somebody is always breaking the crust of custom and there are always leakages around the edges.

There is nothing objectionable about a bureaucratic literature, given a bureaucratic society. It was good that to get a job as a minor executive in the postal service of imperial China you had to turn out a respectable essay on a passage in the Classics and a conventional poem. Some of the best poets of China in the great ages of its literature were generals and statesmen, and almost all were what we would call civil-service employees. America would be a better place if every army officer, postmaster, sanitary engineer, or industrialist, could turn out a nice poem when he took his wife and kiddies for a picnic by the reservoir. This is the long-term objective of academic poetry, of the thousands of courses of creative writing. I have never understood why my colleagues resent it when I point this out. The general tendency of the Establishment is to assimilate the alienated. Only a handful of creative artists in any medium remain unemployable, most especially in a culture like the American, where sensationalism is a prime value and dissent is the hottest commodity on Madison Avenue.

However, since the end of the Second War, one aspect of the technology has permanently shattered the crust of custom for all but the most rigid, and has made all but the most insensitive alienated at least a little. That of course is the Bomb. Hiroshima and Nagasaki permanently warped that elusive conceptual entity, the public mind of the United States, the American soul that once had been dreaming the American dream. America is a guilty nation in which everybody lives in the shadow of apocalypse, and one of the Seven Last Things of the Apocalypse is Judgment. To Baudelaire or Rimbaud, to T. S. Eliot, the end of Western

Civilization may have seemed immanent, but the end of the world did not. This is the difference. That alienation from a society of progress and optimism, that eschatological world-view which has been a tradition of the leading artists and intellectuals of modern Western society, of capitalist civilization, has always had a remote and slightly delusional or neurotic character about it. Was it really happening? Since the sudden end of the Second War eschatology has ceased to be a world-view; it has become a simple fact with which every living person must reckon. This is the difference.

The British Empire, and so, with it, Victorian civilization, never recovered from the mass guilty conscience resulting from the Boer War. Suddenly, added to the burdens of Negro slavery and genocide of the American Indian, the culture-bearers of American civilization were asked to shoulder the devastating load of Nagasaki and Hiroshima. As society's experts in the symbolic criticism of values, American poets began to secede, disaffiliate, go into permanent opposition, to the dominant culture.

At first everything seemed to be going along as usual. The interbellum generation was still in control. There were articles in the quarterlies repeating once again, but even more confidently, "The generation of experiment and revolt is over." "Little magazines full of free verse are an almost forgotten phenomenon." "Nobody goes to Montparnasse anymore. Everybody goes to St. Germain." This difference is simple. The cafés of the Boulevard St. Germain were frequented by middle-aged, successful intellectuals, and they were twice the price of the cheaper ones of Montparnasse, where the habitueés were half the age. It is extraordinary that the editors of the *Partisan Review,* once the organ of the Communist John Reed Clubs, and of revolutionary modernism, could visit the magazine stand of the Gotham Book Mart and pick up a copy of the *Hudson* or *Kenyon Reviews* and literally not see all about them the dozens of little magazines, mimeographed, printed on hand presses, or by job printers, full of free verse and anarchism, but so it was.

At first the change seemed to spread from few centers— San Francisco and Black Mountain College and less conspicuously, the first settlements in what was later to be called the East Village in New York City.

Black Mountain College, buried in the hills of North Carolina, was founded by John Rice, between the wars, in a last upsurge of creative education which produced Bennington and Bard, and affected profound changes in schools like Sarah Lawrence and Briarcliff. Unlike the others, Black Mountain never had enough money to realize the hopes of its founders to pay the going rate for its faculty. Therefore it became a refuge for dedicated pedagogues with most advanced ideas. They each and all seem to have been dedicated to quite different ideas, and in its heyday Black Mountain also was a political battleground of intellectuals who considered themselves Stalinists, Lovestonites, Trotskyites, or Norman Thomas Socialists, but who in the struggles on the tiny campus changed sides with the greatest facility. The final reduction of all the absurdums was a new life style which would converge with that of the worldwide counter culture, after the Second War. Above the battle were a few very important artists and writers whose influence was to be profound on the oncoming generation. Most famous was Joseph Albers, who had been at the Bauhaus, and his wife Anni Albers, once of the finest weavers of modern times, and the anthropologist, Paul Radin. Others came and went and left an enduring mark

133

on the student body. The number of people who went to tiny Black Mountain and who became leading artists, writers, musicians, dancers, and craftsmen after the Second War was out of all proportion to the school's poverty, primitive plant, faction-ridden faculty, and miniscule student body. Bohemia was out of date in Greenwich Village and banished from all literary cocktail parties, but it raised its head again in Black Mountain and established fashions—beards, blue jeans, bare feet or black stockings, free verse, free love, free grass—which later were to be called hip, beat, and hippie.

One of the persons who endured through all the changes was Paul Goodman, who taught at Black Mountain a part of the year for many years. Goodman emerged from the war years a pacifist, and a communitarian anarchist. He was also one of the very few American intellectuals at all connected with the Establishment who was part of the main stream of international modernism—in life attitude, in philosophy, in literary style. Had Goodman written in French he would have been world famous by the time he was thirty. He was a social philosopher, a political analyst, a devoted pedagogue, a poet and dramatist, and a novelist and short-story writer. Twenty-five years after the war the Old Left was still complaining that the New Left was without theory, strategy, tactics, or objectives, and this charge was largely true, except for Paul Goodman, who had continued as the only comprehensive and systematic philosopher in the United States of the libertarian revolt and the secession into an alternative society which was to be the dominant tendency of the second post-war world.

Paul Goodman was the mentor, but never anything resembling an organization leader, of a small libertarian circle in New York out of which amongst other things

134

developed the Living Theater. He was, also rather contradic-
torily, for many years one of the four think tanks of the
ex-Left Establishment around the *Partisan Review* and
Commentary and one of the inspirers of Dwight Mac-
donald's *Politics*. The three others were Edouard Roditi,
Lionel Abel, and Harold Rosenberg, originally poets first
published in *Blues*. Edouard Roditi, who had gone to the
University of Chicago with Goodman, was a considerable
influence on him.

After the war Charles Olson, like Louis Zukofsky, essentially a follower of Ezra Pound of the *Cantos* and William
Carlos Williams of *Paterson,* came to teach at Black Mountain, and after him, Robert Creeley, and then, from the
San Francisco group, Robert Duncan. By this time, being
a teacher or a student at Black Mountain meant considerable sacrifice, because the school had hardly any money
at all. Diet was spartan and the maintenance, secretarial
work, service, and even the cooking were done by students
and faculty. Nevertheless the school kept turning out young
writers and artists who would make a difference in the
years to come. Finally it became impossible to continue.
The property was sold off and the money divided up and
the last little band of faithful staged a sad and lonesome
party and left forever. The poets usually identified with
Black Mountain are Jonathan Williams, Edward Dorn, Paul
Blackburn, Joel Oppenheimer, but in fact the list is immense
and includes people as diverse as Ruth Herschberger and
Jackson MacLow.

XI.

In San Francisco the revolt against the entire culture of the interbellum period was more widely and solidly based than on the East Coast. During the Depression years the labor movement was much more thoroughly radicalized than the rest of the country, and many young writers were drawn into active participation, not just into demonstrations, parades, and "proletarian literature," but into actual trade-union activity. In the northern part of the state the strong libertarian tradition of the Industrial Workers of the World was still alive, although the organization itself had ceased to have but a tiny handful of members. Trade-union and political activity were more free of authoritarianism and bureaucracy than elsewhere, and trade-union racketeering and criminality was scarcely known. In California even the Communist Party was full of mavericks. Left artists' and writers' organizations were proportionately much larger than in New York. In San Francisco there was scarcely a writer or artist who was not at some time involved, and involved in a freer, less doctrinaire fashion than in New York or Chicago. Mass chants, agitprop theater, Lehrstück, blue-blouse dramatic troups, long epic plays about the Paris Commune, the Russian Revolution, John Brown, collective murals of working-class life—racial cultural activities in San Francisco compared favorably with those in pre-

Hitler Berlin. The WPA (work relief) artists, writers, and theater projects were more productive of enduring results than anywhere else in the country.

Perhaps even more important, San Francisco was far away from the literary marketplace. Not only did local poets develop quite independently of the infighting of New York literary cocktail parties, but writers came to Northern California from other parts of the country to escape the factional, ultimately commercial, pressures of the East. Only a small percentage of the poets now identified as the San Francisco school were born in California, and many of them, for instance Ginsberg, have lived there only for short periods.

San Francisco is the only major city in America except New Orleans not colonized by the overland spread of the Puritan ethos. It was settled by the rascally and anarchistic types attracted to any gold rush, by North Italians who soon became one of the elite groups of the city, and by a small number of Jewish families mostly from northern Bavaria, mostly well to do and highly civilized before they migrated to America. Until the city was caught up in the population explosion, the racial conflicts and the crooked politics of the 1960's, it was one of the last homes of *la vie mediterranée*, of personal *laissez faire* and *dolce far niente*, certainly a more Mediterranean city than post-War Two Barcelona, Marseilles, or Genoa.

During the war there were a large number of concentration camps for conscientious objectors scattered through the mountains and forests of the West Coast. On their leaves, these young men came to San Francisco, where they encountered the libertarian, pacifist, group of intellectuals already numbering many of the leading intellectuals of the community. At Waldport on the southern coast of Oregon—as isolated as possible—there was eventually established a conscientious objectors' camp of creative artists of all kinds who had been nothing but insoluable problems to the administration. After the war possibly a majority of these people settled in the San Francisco Bay Area. Out of them came a radio station, three or four theaters, several publishing enterprises, and a number of well-known musicians, painters, and sculptors.

Far Eastern religion, literature, and art were much more accessible in San Francisco, much more naturally come by than in New York. Buddhist temples are commonplace in the cities of California. The influence of Japanese and Chinese culture is direct. After all, the Pacific Ocean is just water; China and Japan are adjacent to California. A thickly populated land mass is a barrier. The ocean, like the inner Asian desert and steppe, is a long bridge. Culturally San Francisco was in closer contact with London and Paris than with New York. Young poets in San Francisco were much more aware of the New Romantics, Apocalyptics, and libertarians in wartime London, and the poets of the Resistance in France, than most writers in New York.

By no means of least importance, after the great organizing drives and strikes of 1934–36, the San Francisco Bay Area rapidly became the highest wage region in the country—for blue-collar workers—but for white-collar workers, wages remained lower than in Chicago, New York, and Washington. It had always been customary for young middle-class people in the West to get summer work in rugged outdoor jobs in agriculture, at sea, and in the forests. So too, older writers could work at a trade-union organized job and make enough money in a few months to live comfortably for the rest of the year. When Allen Ginsberg came to San Francisco he took a hard, dull white-collar job as a market researcher for forty dollars a week. He soon quit it and went to sea on trips into the Arctic Ocean at double pay and made enough money to live for over a year and go around the world as well. These high-wage, genuinely proletarian, opportunities meant that the young San Francisco writer was likely to reach maturity with a far different set of social attitudes from that of his fellow in the East.

All these factors combined to produce a regional culture differing at almost every point from the New York-centered literary world of the rest of America. It was not just a regional renaissance, like the Middle Western, Chicago-centered one of the early years of the century. It was more like the culture of a different country whose inhabitants happened to speak American.

The total lack of commercial market meant that most literary activity took the form of poetry in booklets or little magazines printed on small hand presses, or far more important, read aloud. Poetry readings were a regular feature of the San Francisco Anarchist Circle and were attended by two hundred or more people weekly, and several individuals held weekly seminars and readings in their own homes. The first poets of the now famous San Francisco Renaissance, which everybody, no matter how Johnny-Come-Lately, thinks began with him, were Robert Duncan, Philip Lamantia, Jack Spicer, and Brother Antoninus, then and now William Everson. All were conscientious objectors, Duncan, heroically enough, after he had got in the Army. Everson taught himself to be one of the country's finest printers on an ancient press at Waldport. During and immediately after the war other people began to appear. Kenneth Patchen moved to San Francisco. Henry Miller lived in Big Sur. Although, contrary to common opinion, Henry Miller had almost no personal contact with San Francisco writers, he certainly added to the liberating climate.

Three little magazines of that period—*Circle,* edited by George Leite; *City Lights,* edited then by Pete Martin (the son of the famous anarchist Carlo Tresca who was assassinated in New York on the eve of the war); and *The Ark,* published by the San Francisco Anarchist Circle—not officially; it did nothing officially, even collect dues, or have officers, or even a meeting chairman—were the first clear, organized expression of the international post-War Two culture on this side of the Atlantic.

Around 1948 Lawrence Ferlinghetti came to San Francisco from Paris and bought City Lights Bookshop from Pete Martin. James Broughton, Madeleine Gleason, Jack Spicer, Lew Welch, Robert Duncan, Philip Lamantia, were all working in San Francisco then. Other people gathered around—Michael McClure, John Weiners, Ron Loewinsohn, David Meltzer, Kirby Doyle, Lenore Kandel, and little magazines and poetry readings proliferated in all directions.

All of these people have appeared frequently on the cooperative radio station KPFA, founded by the late Louis Hill, a poet and a former member of the National Board for Conscientious Objectors. KPFA has been the single most powerful cultural influence in the Bay Area.

Another was the San Francisco Poetry Center, founded by Madeleine Gleason with the assistance of Robert Duncan and myself and shortly thereafter housed by San Francisco State College and managed by Ruth Witt Diamant, a woman as dedicated and self-sacrificing as ever was

Harriet Monroe, and considerably more open-minded. Both these institutions, incidentally, were enabled to rise to their full potentialities due to large grants from the Rockefeller Foundation.

In 1956 and '57 Allen Ginsberg, Gregory Corso, and Jack Kerouac showed up in San Francisco. Up until that time Ginsberg had been a rather conventional, witty poet influenced by his New Jersey *Landsman* William Carlos Williams, and taught his letters at Columbia by Mark Van Doren, Lionel Trilling, and Jacques Barzun. He was very much a catecumen of the highly select Trotskyite-Southern Agrarian Establishment, and destined by his elders to step into the thinning ranks of their youth brigade alongside Norman Podhoretz and Susan Sontag and others of like ilk and kidney. He inhaled the libertarian atmosphere of San Francisco and exploded. He took part in the now historic reading at the Six Gallery, along with Michael McClure, Lamantia, Ferlinghetti, and myself, and two young men just down from Reed College in Oregon, Gary Snyder and Philip Whalen. He read *Howl* and started an epoch.

What happened in San Francisco first and spread from there across the world was public poetry, the return of a tribal, preliterate relationship between poet and audience. There are today in San Francisco more poetry readings in a week than anyone can keep track of and still more people writing lyrics for rock groups. Granted that this stuff is not of the very highest literary quality judged by the standards of now forgotten mentors like John Crowe Ransom, but it is the beginning of an artistic activity which pervades, in fact, saturates, its ever growing subculture.

It is significant that what the world thinks of as the San Francisco scene is almost completely dominated by poetry.

141

McClure, Duncan, Ferlinghetti, and I have written plays. There are very few novels and even less criticism. Alan Watts lives in Marin Country, and has had a profound influence on younger people thereabouts. For years he delivered the Sunday sermon on KPFA.

In New York the post-war break with the past occurred first in painting. Abstract Expressionism, America's first original contribution to the development of modern painting, was a rejection at every point of the Cubist, geometrical abstract, classicist, tradition that had ruled the arts since Cezanne and Seurat. The Abstract Expressionist painters considered a painting not as a painting *of* something, not even of abstract forms, but insisted upon presenting it directly as a painted surface, an object in its own right which showed forth, not the archetectonic "significant form" of the previous two generations, but the direct expression in the material of paint of the personality of the artist in action. The only well-known previous painting of this kind had been the early work of Kandinsky.

Several of the leaders of the movement had developed their new style just after the war while teaching in San Francisco at the California School of Fine Arts, then under the adventurous directorship of Douglas McAgy. Clyfford Still, Mark Rothko, and others were leaders of a well-developed school of painting before they migrated to New York, and the ancestor of the movement, Arshile Gorky, had lived for a long period in San Francisco between the wars, as had John Ferren. Most of the members of the self-styled New York School of Poets were personal friends of the Abstract Expressionists, frequented the Cedar Bar and later The White Horse and the Five Spot, went to parties on Tenth Street, and attended meetings of the Abstract

Expressionist discussion group "The Club," and wrote about their painter friends in *Art News* and *The Arts*.

Except for the Scot, Ruthven Todd, who had emigrated to America, actually the poets were far less personalist, expressionist, or neo-romantic than the painters. On the contrary, their principal influences seem to have been the French poets associated with the Cubists, especially Apollinaire and Cocteau, the early "modernistic" Auden, when he himself was learning from Laura Riding, and William Carlos Williams. This is certainly a "classicist" list. What distinguished Kenneth Koch, John Ashbery, Barbara Guest, Frank O'Hara, James Schuyler from the classicists of the Reactionary Generation was their escape from provincialism. This was literally as well as literarily true. Most of them lived for fairly long periods in Europe and were accepted by the rather glittering world of permanent expatriates and lady art patrons of which Paul Bowles and Peggy Guggenheim are familiar examples—the more cultivated and well-to-do survivors of interbellum Paris-America. Most of them were published in Margaret Caetani's *Botteghe Oscura*. As a group their poetry is characterized by witty sophistication, and is distinguished from the work of the San Francisco people by its lack of overt serious social concern. In comparison with Robert Duncan or Allen Ginsberg they could easily be called frivolous.

Chicago, once the capital of the most vital regional renaissance in America, had produced little of enduring significance for many years, and after World War II, Midwestern literature no longer centered on any one city and lost its strong regional, or provincial, character. Ann Arbor and Detroit, with the Universities of Michigan and Wayne State, Notre Dame University at South Bend, Indiana, the

University of Chicago, from whence came *The Chicago Review* and then out of that *The Big Table Review,* and the writers' workshop at the University of Iowa, all were centers of creative activity.

The place of the *Black Mountain Review* was taken by Cid Corman's *Origin,* which he printed from his income on the GI Bill, or from teaching English in the Kyoto YMCA or from other meager sources, and gave away. No poetry magazine has ever been better edited. *Origin* is a basic documentation of these years.

Probably the leading magazine of the period, *The Fifties* and then *The Sixties,* was published by Robert Bly in Minnesota with no connections with any academic institution. Above all editors of poetry magazines in America, Robert Bly was most conscious of a responsibility to return American poetry to the main stream of international literature, to what the Reactionary Generation had called "the bygone and better forgotten age of experiment and revolt." (Picasso once said, "I never make experiments," and there is certainly nothing experimental about the poetry of Paul Éluard, Octavio Paz, or Georg Trakl. What are experimental are the archaizing provincial experimentations of Baroque verse of the Reactionary Generation.)

Although unfocussed in any school, the list of Midwestern poets of this generation is imposing: Saint Geraud (Bill Knott), Galway Kinnell, Robert Kelly, John Logan, Robert Lax, Paul Carroll, James Wright, Philip Levine. Galway Kinnell is actually a New Englander but has been associated with Bly and the Chicago group.

Of an older generation Theodore Roethke, William Stafford, John Berryman, and Weldon Kees were all born in the Midwest, but could hardly be called regional poets. The native earth that had once nourished Sandburg or

144

Vachel Lindsay or Edgar Lee Masters had ceased to bear its special fruit. One element of the Midwestern tradition still lingered. With the exception of Roethke, Berryman, and Stafford, these Midwest poets all share a much stronger sense of social responsibility and a vatic calling than do the New York or Black Mountain groups. It would be easy to say that this is due to the influence of Weldon Kees and Kenneth Patchen, but it is doubtful if most of them read either one, except casually. Amongst the Midwestern poets, Notre Dame and Loyola University in Chicago provided at least physical centers for a small group of Catholic poets of radically modern sensibility. Dan Berrigan, John Logan, and Robert Lax are examples.

British critics have distinguished a definite school of American verse—Robert Lowell, Theodore Roethke, Sylvia Plath, James Wright, John Berryman, and a number of others whom they call the Confessional School, poets who have recorded profound psychological conflicts or mental breakdown. To this list should be added, above all others, Weldon Kees, to whom the horrors of *The Waste Land,* or W. H. Auden's ruined England in a new Dark Ages, were not literary conventions, but ever present reality, alive and malignant. Weldon Kees disappeared during a mental breakdown in 1955, almost certainly having jumped from the Golden Gate Bridge. He was a profoundly moving poet, playwright, and painter, and an influence on the early days of the formation of the group in San Francisco, where he lived the last years of his life.

Speaking of regional poetry—the South in this period produced little of importance. Apparently once the myth of the Southern physiocratic aristocracy of the Fugitives-Southern Agrarians had become absurd, there was nothing to take its place, nothing to give the White South the cultural coherence that produces significant poets. It is astonishing that in the long drawn-out civil-rights struggle of the Fifties and Sixties, so few white poets were moved to significant utterance—or to utterance at all. The important Southern poets in ever increasing numbers of these years are black.

XII.

IDEALLY, Black poets should be discussed as they occur chronologically, or in "literary schools," on equal terms with everybody else, and their color should not even need mentioning. Many of the poets of the Harlem Renaissance of the Twenties resented being categorized as Negro poets. This was especially true of Jean Toomer and Countee Cullen. After the Second War in the early days of desegregation and integration this attitude was common again. Very few people knew that Gloria Oden was a Negro until long after she had become widely published. In the Sixties with the growth of a new, militant separatism and the demand for purely Black critical standards and the mystique of Black esthetics—"Black is Beautiful"—and the popularity of the notion that white people cannot possibly understand African sculpture, jazz and gospel music, and Black literature, many Black poets today insist upon being categorized, being treated as essentially a cultural expression of a conquered country within the borders of the United States. So perhaps it is best to treat the poetry of the American Negro in a separate chapter.

Before doing so it should be pointed out that the intensity of feelings about *négritude* and Black nationalism may well pass, as integration demanded by the economy proceeds in spite of either Black or White prejudice. The

147

same is true of the use of the word "Black" itself. The Black radicals of the Twenties and Thirties propagandized tirelessly to do away with the many evasions and euphemisms —"Afro-American" and "colored," and a dozen others, some of them fantastic and absurd—used to designate members of their race, and to substitute the one word "Negro"—capitalized. They had no sooner got their way against the resistence of the bulk of the older people who had insisted on calling themselves "colored," than the next generation said that Negro was a white man's term of contempt, like nigger, and that the proper term was Black—capitalized. The same thing incidentally has gone on in France and French-speaking Africa where *Noir,* which was in fact a white man's term of contempt, is now insisted upon in preference to the neutral *nègre.* To the sympathetic white man all this quarrelling over terminology seems unimportant, especially since the majority of American Blacks are not in fact Black at all, but colored; and some, like Angela Davis and Kathleen Cleaver, for instance, would not be considered Negroes in any other country in history or on earth. Both are in fact less black than Pushkin or the elder Dumas.

There is something to be said for an esthetic of *négritude,* or perhaps now we should call it *Noirétude:* in a country where white faces are used to advertise everything and white figures are the models of status and prestige, and writing, painting, and music by white people are presented to everybody indiscriminately as the examples to be imitated, it is essential that the American Black, whose sense of his identity and cultural rootedness were crippled by slavery, should regain that confidence which comes from a sense of community and continuity. On the other hand negritude is no excuse for poor work, cheap melodrama, sentimentality, and sterile propaganda, however militant. Vicious anti-Semitic doggerel is vicious doggerel, whether it's written by a Black American or a White German or by Ezra Pound or e. e. cummings.

There is one factor, however, which might seem an excuse, but which is not, and which must be well understood before one approaches a judgment of Black American poetry. Most Black writers do not come from the special elite culture, itself quite segregated, of the American intellectuals. They come from the mass culture and share its style and standards, even when they transcend them. For this reason most Black poets have been more conventional than white ones. The militants' charge that Black America is an internal colony has been true as far as poetry was concerned. Black poetry has been provincial, like Canadian, until recent years, or Australian still. Of course it's quite possible to be provincial and good. The judgment is really a sociological one, but it can be easily confused with a value judgment.

These considerations may account for the comparative lack of provincialism in the poetry of Black South Africa where the race certainly suffers from greater disabilities than it does in most of America, and in African poetry in the French language, which at the present moment is probably superior to that by most white Frenchmen, who seem to be becoming provincial imitators of Yvor Winters at the best, or Archibald MacLeish. Black Africa has never lost its sense of cultural continuity and today everybody is aware that African accomplishments in music and sculpture are the equal of any in the world. In addition the South African Bantu know well that they are the inheritors of a

149

heroic past. The descendents of the Zulu and Matabele chieftains are not tempted to yield to self-pity and sentimentality.

Black American poetry is almost as old as white. In 1746 a slave girl, Lucy Terry, published a little epic, *Bars Fight,* the story of an Indian raid on Deerfield. In 1773 Phillis Wheatley became famous in both America and England with her *Poems on Various Subjects, Religious and Moral.* She was born in Senegal, sold into slavery, and brought to Boston in 1761. Very soon she had learned to read and write. She was only seventeen when she published "A Poem by Phillis, a Negro Girl in Boston, on the Death of the Reverend George Whitefield." She developed tuberculosis and her doctor advised her to take a long sea voyage, so she went to England, where her book was published. She returned to the States, married, and died in obscure poverty.

Although they are perennial heroines of Negro History Week, neither of these young women wrote very good verses. The remarkable thing was that they wrote at all. Both were enslaved to Northern families who treated them well and encouraged their education, and Phillis Wheatley was given her freedom. In the South after the first slave rebellions it became illegal in most states to teach a slave, and in some cases, simply a Negro, to read and write. As time went on freedmen, freemen—the small class of Negroes born free, and many literate house slaves fled to the North and eventually to Canada. Those who did not, like Frederick Douglass and John Mercer Langston, devoted themselves to bettering the lot of their people, a more pressing need than *belles lettres.*

There were plenty of literate Negroes in Louisiana and in some of the former French towns of the Mississippi drainage, but they wrote in French. Furthermore, they were rather sharply divided into illiterate Blacks and literate "creoles of color," until the Eighties when Reconstruction was dismantled and the colored elite were dispossessed and driven into the Black community. It was out of this fusing of the two groups that musically literate New Orleans jazz arose—"My folks was all Frenchmens," said Jelly Roll Morton.

Jupiter Hammon, George Moses Horton, Lucy Terry, wrote in slavery and their verses cannot compete with the poetry of the white culture, however hard they try. Black culture found its expression as folk culture in tales like those altered and adapted for white consumption by Joel Chandler Harris as "Uncle Remus," in spirituals, many of which were scarcely concealed songs of revolt or even, as in "Follow the Milk Dipper," coded instructions and directions for escape to the North, and in work songs like "John Henry," and shouts and hollers. The blues, as we know them today, cannot be traced back much beyond the beginning of this century, but narrative ballads, like "Frankie and Albert," "Stagalee," "Big Jim," seem always to have been sung, at least by urban Blacks. The lyrics of all these songs are more important as poetry than anything written by Black Americans until modern times. Black American music and song is perhaps America's most important contribution to world culture, certainly it is the only one taken seriously by many people in other countries—with the possible exception of Whitman. The importance, the all-pervasiveness and intensity, of the role of folk song in the submerged culture of the Negro established an idiom which today gives the young Black American poet closer connections, deeper roots, in his community than are available to most white writers. LeRoi Jones may say, "I am alienated on inspection," but he means from white culture and West-

151

ern Civilization. This is the reason for the rejection of the term "Negro," which the young *négritude* writers apply to the *asimilados,* those colored gentlemen and ladies who have adapted themselves to the white culture, bypassing the huge number of alienated white writers, but who have also alienated themselves from the Black community. The measure of their success is the ability of the writers of *négritude* thoroughly to absorb and to elevate into new realms of significance the folk idiom and the folk attitudes which they claim as their inheritance.

Paul Lawrence Dunbar was, significantly, the son of slaves, but born in freedom. His complete poems were published in 1913 and have been continuously popular ever since. A large proportion of them are in dialect, and reflect the white man's image of the watermelon-stealin', possum-eatin', banjo-thumpin', dancin' and laughin' negra. They must make extremely difficult reading for a young disciple of LeRoi Jones, yet they are worth reading. Behind the minstrel-show mask there speaks an instransigent equalitarian, who if he modelled himself on any white writer, it was Burns, and whose narrative poems do reveal something of the life of the plantation South. Dunbar died young. James Weldon Johnson, born a year earlier, 1871, lived until 1938, and the Harlem Renaissance liberated him from both dialect verse and the refined poetry of the *asimilado.* His *God's Trombones* is probably the most popular book of poetry with ordinary, educated American Negroes ever written. Angelina W. Grimké, Anne Spencer, Georgia Douglas Johnson, all wrote before the First War, were no better, no worse than most white women poets of the time, and Black poetry as such reappears only with Fenton Johnson. He was the son of a wealthy colored family in Chicago and one of the leading members of the Chicago Rennaissance of the early Twenties. His family lost their money in the economic crisis of 1929 and his poetry became harder and more revolutionary, although even in his earlier poems he had made himself a spokesman of the urban poor, the washerwomen, the unemployed, the hustlers and grifters.

The Harlem Renaissance began when the Negro magazines *The Crisis* and *Opportunity* opened their pages to the new poetry being written by young Blacks and when the Jamaican poet, Claude McKay, became an editor of *The Liberator,* successor to *The Masses,* and in fact the "cultural organ" of the Workers' Party. W. E. B. DuBois (pronounced DuBoyce, not DuBwa!) believed passionately that the Negro should put his best foot forward and resisted what he considered the tendency of poets like Langston Hughes, Countee Cullen, and others, to "show the Race at its worst." However, he published their milder poems in *The Crisis,* which was the organ of the NAACP, and so reached a wide and varied audience.

Jean Toomer, the most remarkable poet of the period, was very light, came from a family of well-educated, successful Washington bureaucrats. He was the grandson of P. B. S. Pinchback, Negro acting governor of Louisiana, elected to the Senate but denied his seat. Most of Jean Toomer's friends were white. He was a member of *The Seven Arts,* Stieglitz circle and his principal influence was Waldo Frank and perhaps Sherwood Anderson, both of whom, perhaps, he influenced in turn, for their stories of Negro life indicate careful reading of Jean Toomer. Toomer is the first poet to unite folk culture and the elite culture of the white avant-garde, and he accomplishes this difficult task with considerable success. He is without doubt the most important Black poet, although he was practically white and easily passed, until recent years.

Melvin B. Tolson tried to do a similar thing with his *Libretto for the Republic of Liberia*, published with an insufferably patronizing preface by Col. Allen Tate. Most of his poetry is conventional and sentimental, and the *Libretto* seems only more pretentious, although certainly his sentiments of Black protest are estimable. The only really successfully assimilated poet of this period is Arna Bontemps. The poetry he chooses to be represented by in anthologies has little to do with race, at least overtly, although he has written considerable Black revolutionary poetry in the past. His work is highly skilled, quiet, memorable. He has managed to make himself a gentleman of letters, untrammeled by disabilities of race or nationalities, and could be compared to Witter Bynner or Babette Deutsch. People like him, of any color, are not common in American literature.

Although Black poetry of the period was dominated by Claude McKay, Countee Cullen, and Langston Hughes, the conventional early twentieth-century style, rather like the English Georgian poets, in spite of its passionately delivered racial content, makes the poetry of Claude McKay and Countee Cullen difficult reading for modern tastes, and only Langston Hughes survives. And in his case it is difficult for many people, especially white people, to accept his surface simplicity and ingenuousness. Here we really do run into the question of a *négritude* esthetic. Langston Hughes was the first Black American poet completely to immerse himself in folk speech and to write of and for ordinary Black people. For years he was rejected by the Negro elite "for portraying the worst aspects of the race." His books were read mostly by white people and he had readings in white colleges long before he did in Black ones. After the Second War the tide turned and he became as popular with his race as Carl Sandburg, whom he somewhat resembles,

154

was with his. Langston Hughes came from a well-to-do, well-educated family, spent many of his early years outside the United States, and was later widely traveled and a member of the international literary community, yet no Black poet before him spoke so truly for the poor and semi-literate actual residents of Harlem. The Harlem Renaissance, as he pointed out, was largely a matter of white parties at the homes of the Negro rich, night clubs, and a few coffee shops in imitation of white Greenwich Village—where in fact most of the members of the Renaissance lived.

When he was a young radical member of the Chicago John Reed Club, Richard Wright wrote a number of impressive poems, some of them of protest and revolt, in a long, free-verse line, others, a series of *haiku* which he called "hokku" and which are amongst the very few successful imitations of the Japanese form in any Western language, totally lacking in the coyness and sentimentality of most *haiku* in English including most of the translations of the Japanese. Wright's poetry should be gathered up and republished. No other Black poet of the Red Thirties has survived. On the other hand Robert Hayden, who assimilated the idiom of contemporary modernism much more successfully than Tolson did in his *Libretto,* still writes, and is still read, and is still one of the leading Black poets.

Owen Dodson was the first of the post-War Two poets of the new New Negro, successor to the New Negro of the Harlem Renaissance. He has written poems of protest against war and racism usually conventional in form and significantly, a dirge for the death of Charlie Parker, the great jazz musician. Gwendolyn Brooks started out to write poetry of the ordinary young girl, wife, and mother, to whom her race was only incidental, sometimes annoying, sometimes the occasion for pride. As time has gone on and the conflict in America has deepened and become irreconcilable and the program of pacifist resistance and integration has failed, her poetry has become far more militant and sometimes freer in form. With her own race she is certainly the most popular poet writing today, and so has replaced Langston Hughes, as she has replaced Carl Sandburg as the poet of Chicago and even the Poet Laureate of the state of Illinois. Almost exactly the same things that I have said about Langston Hughes, both style and content, can be said about Gwendolyn Brooks.

There are a number of poets in the early post-war period who write competent, careful, conventional verse. Margaret Walker; Frank Yerby, the very successful novelist; Carl Holman, Margaret Danner, who were successful at adapting themselves to white standards but who are not as such very outstanding. The most successfully assimilated of all was Gloria C. Oden, who as I mentioned earlier was well-established as a contributor to *Poetry* and the *Saturday Review* and other magazines long before anybody knew that G. C. Oden was either a girl or a Negro. "Otherwise how would I ever know if I could write at all?" said she. In recent years she too has been caught up in the new consciousness of race, of the importance of Black culture, and of the necessity for Black militancy.

There were three Black poets associated with the cultural overturn of the Beat Generation—Robert Kaufman, Ted Joans, and LeRoi Jones. Of mixed parentage, light in color, and with Caucasian features, Bob Kaufman, although he is in a sense a militant revolutionary in both art and politics, does not seem to think of himself as a Negro, much less a Black in capital letters. Unfortunately he publishes very little, but his two books, *Solitudes Crowded with Loneliness* and *Golden Sardine,* are amongst the best product of the Beat Generation. Ted Joans, the oldest of the three, has always seemed to me to be to Kaufman and LeRoi Jones as Rod McKuen is to Allen Ginsberg.

LeRoi Jones' career marks the turning point in Black poetry after the Second War. He started out apparently completely identified, not with the white culture of the Establishment, but with the counter culture. With Diane Di Prima he edited the magazine *The Floating Bear,* and later his own magazine, *Yugen.* He was a Buddhist, pacifist, and anarchist, married to a white girl and the father of a family, who loved all sentient creatures. He had become accepted as the leading Negro poet of the new avant-garde. Suddenly he began to change into a kind of secular Black Muslim, a violent Black nationalist and anti-Semite and the leader of an Africanist ashram and the founder of Harlem's Black Arts Theater. A great deal of his later poetry is a direct exhortation, not just to armed revolt, but to violent hatred of all white people, but especially Jews. His influence on young Black militant writers was for a while very great, but as the experience of the Black Muslims and the Black Panthers has caused them to cool their exhortations to indiscriminate racist violence his more inflammatory poems have lost some of their appeal. Since LeRoi Jones himself comes from by Negro standards a privileged, professional family, was raised in the suburbs, went through the university, and has received many honors and awards, his most virulent poetry seems forced and artificial. Some people have called it psychotic, and others, "objectively the work of a provocateur." It certainly is not as good as his earlier work, which never strove for easy effects, and was never marred by sentimentality, melodrama, and self-pity, the besetting sins of not just Black militants, but of the work of any oppressed group which can always rely on the automatic approval of a claque. At his best LeRoi Jones is certainly one of the major Black writers, the equal of Jean Toomer, Richard Wright and Ralph Ellison, Langston Hughes and Gwendolyn Brooks, all of whom, one would judge from his recent work, he heartily despises. Certainly his work appeals more to white audiences, except for a limited number of young Black, intellectual militants, than it does to ordinary Negroes, who find his later poetry, like his remarkable plays, offensive because they "portray the worst aspects of the race," with, in every sense, a vengeance!

LeRoi Jones, like Langston Hughes before him, has been a tireless promoter of younger, undiscovered, Black poets, but in his case, only those he agrees with. There has been an explosion of Black poetry in America, much like all the other explosions. There are courses in Black studies and in Black poetry in colleges all over the country, and publishers find a ready market for an endless stream of anthologies, the more militant the better. There are now so many good young Black poets that it is impossible to keep track of them. Those that have impressed me most have been, first, some remarkable young women—Julia Fields, Nikki Giovanni, Sonia Sanchez, Carole Gregory, Kattie M. Cumbo, Alicia Loy Johnson. There seems to be a disproportionate number of good Black women poets, a reflection of the privileged position of Black women, both in their own society and in relation to the white world, and this is reflected in the greater calm and confidence with which they write. They seem to be much less subject to a common fault in the poetry of young, Black, militant men, a certain rattledness and nervous tension, like that of troops under fire, but this does not mean that there are not plenty of good poets amongst them. Those I am familiar with and like are Charles Cooper, Lance Jeffers, William J. Harris,

James Arlington Jones, Richard M. Thomas, Sun Ra, Calvin C. Hernton, Ed Bullins, Joe Goncalves, Welton Smith, Larry Neal, Alden Van Buskirk, Clarence Major, Sotere Torregian.

With few exceptions Black poets of this generation write in a contemporary idiom. Some of them, like Sun Ra and Goncalves, are very far out indeed. Yet there is a difference. They do not write modelling themselves on the contemporary white avant-garde as did Tolson or Hayden, but more like Jean Toomer, they attempt, sometimes successfully, sometimes not, to assimilate the folk inheritance to the international idiom; and usually it is the dominance of the mind and rhythm of the folk culture which makes their verse good. It is not echoes of Paul Éluard and García Lorca or even Nicholas Guillen or Sédar Senghor that matter, but the background music of three hundred years of songs of protest and inner freedom. This is something that can't be faked. Not every elegy on the death of Charlie Parker shows any sense of the meaning of his music.

XIII.

THIS brings us to the Seventies, to the people who would be the new generation of the new decade, but before considering them it would be good to take a backward look over the years since 1955, the beginning of a great change in American poetry. Later by a few years the same thing happened in poetry that had happened in painting. The Abstract Expressionists developed not just a new school, or a new style, but a new attitude toward painting—action painting—and a new attitude toward the painting as product, no longer a picture of something, but a painted surface, an object in its own right. Abstract Expressionism became the dominant art form throughout the world and held this position about fifteen years—the first time American painting had ever had any international influence at all.

Music too was going through a revolution. The modern music which had developed from Schoenberg's twelve-tone scale was really just another form of Romantic music, Brahms brought up to date with a new system of harmony and melodic structure that turned out to be not so new after all, and was far sooner exhausted than the ways of doing music that had developed from Bach and Handel. All over the world, but especially in America and Germany, musicians began to say music is simply what composers do with sound and musical compositions are sounds in time to be considered as such in their own right. Modernist composers had been working with new musical resources since before the First War, but they were few and far between. Suddenly young musicians everywhere seemed to remember Edgar Varese, the Russian Futurists, the young George Antheil, and the early experimentations with electronic music, with devices like the theremin ("Cristobal Colon"—an old Columbia record)—found music—*musique concrète,* made up of taped natural sounds, electronic music of all sorts, the use of exotic instruments from all cultures, the use of all sorts of resonant things as instruments, the abandonment of the musical score, the development of new ways of writing music, and a new emphasis on improvisation. In the twenty years after the Second World War, contemporary music changed past recognition, at least by the previous generation of young disciples of Schoenberg and Stravinsky. Today the most active and influential musicians seem to come from the United States, Germany, and Japan —the same, incidentally, is true of painters.

It took longer for things to get started in poetry. The Establishment was much more entrenched. It was impossible for the new generation whose existence the Establishment denied to get published until they were able to finance their own publication. The Establishment controlled the market and the market was very small indeed. The least of the Beat poets would far outsell the most famous Establishmentarians. There was only a minute audience for the conventional imitators of the classic modernists and justly so. It was necessary for a new generation to develop a new audience and this was done in the first instance by poetry readings, not by books and magazines.

As in painting and music the change was in the medium. In fact, it was a change of medium—poetry as voice not as printing. The climacteric was not the publication of a book,

161

it was the famous Six Gallery reading, the culmination of twenty years of the oral presentation of poetry in San Francisco. Note that the hosts were a cooperative of then very young post-Abstract Expressionist painters who greeted the performance with joy. In the same year Kenneth Patchen, Lawrence Ferlinghetti, and myself were doing poetry to jazz all over the country. It didn't really matter if the *Hudson Review* printed us or not, and it never would have occurred to us to try.

Looking back over those years what were the results, what were the important poems, who were the important poets?

I think they were Denise Levertov, Allen Ginsberg, Lawrence Ferlinghetti, Robert Duncan, Robert Creeley, Gregory Corso, Charles Olson, Philip Lamantia, Kenneth Koch, Frank O'Hara, John Ashbery, Philip Whalen, and coming up as a slightly younger generation, Gary Snyder, Michael McClure, LeRoi Jones, and David Meltzer. Today these people are established if not members of a new Establishment. Most of them in their turn are teaching at a university, although some have remained preternaturally unassimilable and they have a half generation of accomplishment or more behind them. I think it can safely be said that they compare favorably with the heroic age of the classic American modernists who appeared in *Others, The Little Review, Broom, The Egoist,* and *transition.* Not only that but they are not alone. The gap between Eliot, Pound, Williams, and about ten other people and everybody else writing poetry in English at the time was enormous, whereas the generation of the Fifties and Sixties includes a second team of poets of high accomplishment which could be expanded indefinitely. Partly this is just due to the population explosion and the education explosion and the new leisure, but these social and economic factors have conspired to produce a democratization of art unparalleled in history.

Contrary to popular opinion an outstanding characteristic of this group, the avant-garde of the Fifties and Sixties, is its catholicity. They are more unlike each other than were T. S. Eliot and William Carlos Williams. Denise Levertov, for instance, is perhaps the most accomplished of all. She is commonly linked with the Beats or the Black Mountains, never with the New York Group where her place is taken by Barbara Guest, yet she really bears no resemblance to Robert Creeley or Allen Ginsberg and her poetry would have been perfectly acceptable since 1920, and if it had been French, since 1900.

The contrast between Denise Levertov and the women poets of the early part of the century is startling. In comparison with her poetry, theirs makes being a woman in itself at the best a form of neurasthenia. Denise Levertov writes at ease as a woman about love, marriage, motherhood, deaths in the family. The universal round of domestic life is transformed by the sensibility and moved into the transcendent setting of "wholeness, harmony, and radiance," yet this is only a portion of her work, a group of subjects lying naturally to hand and left easily for other subjects as diverse as can be—poems of social protest, of nature, of meditation and contemplation, of vision. The last three categories are the experience of a visionary at home in the world, with a wider range of knowledge and more different kinds of experience than most poets, let alone most women poets in the past. It's almost invidious to so accentuate her sex, but it is very significant because her poetry, in a far different sense from that of the distraught contributors to *Pagan,* is a poetry of sexual liberation of a human person moving freely in the world.

All the poets of this generation are distinguished by a quest for direct, interpersonal communication. Speech from one human to another. Denise Levertov's style is characterized by its low visibility. Her poems are so carefully wrought that the workmanship goes by unnoticed. They seem like speech, heightened and purified. Although her poems are modernistic enough to satisfy any avant-garde editor of the Twenties, they are certainly never obscure, never seem to be doing anything but communicating with presentational immediacy.

The best, the earlier, poetry of Robert Creeley is exactly the opposite. It is about the inability to communicate, an inability due to corruption of the organs of reciprocity. For Robert Creeley the interpersonal "force field" as they call it in physics is so distorted and damaged that only remote, token signals can be pushed across it with the greatest effort. What is the source of this failure of communication? Power, exploitation, subjection, and finally the doubt that there is an Other, and a fear that there is, and the fear that there is not. As Creeley has become more adjusted to life in a mysterious and evil world, his poetry has declined. Its great virtue was its existential guilt, and as this leaves it, what remains is a polished, refined, minute objectivism in a verse of wavering sensitivity. What is there? Is it there or not? The poetry most like it is Mallarmé's little epigrams of the sensibility—"Petit air" or "Un Autre éventail" or certain modern Japanese *waka*.

Philip Lamantia has lived much of his adult life abroad, in France, Spain, Tangiers, Mexico, and for many years enjoyed a more considerable reputation there than in America. He is the youngest member of the second, or is it the third generation of Surrealists, a literary contemporary of René Daumal, Georges Schéhadé, Henri Pichette, Aimé

Cesaire, and an immediate predecessor of the cosmic, meta-physical, and religious revolutionary poets who came to prominence in France after the Second War. In an age when visions can be bought ready cooked in the Monoprix and Prisunic, Lamantia stands out from all the others. There is nothing induced about his visionary poetry. The language of vision is his most natural speech. A great deal of what has happened since in poetry was anticipated in the poetry Lamantia wrote before he was twenty-one. Of all the people in the San Francisco group his is the work which should have the widest appeal to the counter culture, the youth revolt that took form in the Sixties. Unfortunately, for a long period it was inaccessible, published in small editions or in foreign magazines and anthologies. Beginning with *Selected Poems* in the City Lights Pocket Poets series he began to be discovered by young people who until then had never heard of him.

Robert Duncan has always stood in the mid-channel of the main stream of international modernism. At times he has deliberately imitated the old masters— André Breton, Gertrude Stein, James Joyce, Tristan Tzara, and the rest. And he has written political revolutionary poetry like Louis Aragon at his best, such as the latter's "Front Rouge." It would be possible to make up an anthology of all the important trends in modern poetry from Duncan's work. This is not an unfavorable criticism. Duncan's output has been enormous and he can afford to parade briefly his influences. Certainly he has learned from them. He is a man of many skills with a full orchestra of poetic instruments at his disposal. In addition there is a great deal going on in his poetry, intellectually as well as, shall we say, imagistically. Duncan is given to spending a whole season mining a philosophical attitude or a symbolic system in series of poems

165

derived from the Kabbalah or the *I Ching* or Alfred North Whitehead or Rosa Luxemburg or whomever. A great deal of the material of his poetry has since become very fashionable, but like Lamantia, he was using it long before other people.

Lawrence Ferlinghetti is one of a trio of remarkably similar poets of social satire—with Raymond Queneau and Jacques Prévert. Doubtless they have influenced one another but their similarity is due to basic attitudes, to the way they respond to the contemporary world. All three are *engagé* in a way that poets like Lamantia and Duncan are not. Many contemporary poets, perhaps the most significant ones, have simply left the society, deserted it as doomed, or already dead. Ferlinghetti is very much inside it. He feels its evils as directed against him; as they say, he takes it personally. A blood-drunk ruler of a great nation is a personal insult to him. The rapacity of American imperialism is doing something to him. He is there. He sees the napalm fall. He hears the jokes in the locker room. He is the man on the street. To many poets of the counter culture all this seems to be happening to another species as it is rushing itself to extinction, but not Ferlinghetti. He cannot understand why his fellow men have gone mad and yet he can—because he is the only humorous poet of the San Francisco group. Many of his poems are deliberately funny. Gallows humor, I suppose, is a symptom of the deepest sympathy for mankind. At its best his poetry, more than anybody else's, captures the rhythms of modern jazz, perhaps because he shares so many of the deeper life attitudes of the best jazz musicians.

By sheer massive insistence, he was over six and a half feet tall, heavy set, and abnormally vigorous, Charles Olson made himself the theoretician and mentor of the Black Mountain group. People came from all over the country to study with him and as the place declined he was at last all there was left, and closed the school, and sold off and divided the money amongst the trustees. He was as massive and compulsive a writer as he was a man, the master of a singularly heavy prose. What his theories sum up to really is the objectivism of Louis Zukofsky and William Carlos Williams and a prosody based on the cadence, the breath strophe, whether natural or induced by unconventional breaks in the line. There is nothing here that was not in H.D. The test is practice, and in practice Olson turns out to have had a heavy and conventional ear. In a famous statement on what he called "projective verse," "projective," that is, strophic, he quotes "Westron wynde" in an exceptionally flattened and modernized version which completely destroys the haunting rhythm of the original and which cannot be sung syllable for syllable to the melody.

The Tudor music manuscript goes:

> Westron wynde when wilt thou blow:
> The smalle rain down can rayne.
> Crist that my love were in my armys:
> I in my bed agayne.

Olson's version, which he uses to demonstrate the relation of syllable to line and line as strophe, "the HEAD, by way of the EAR, to the SYLLABLE. The HEART, by way of the BREATH, to the LINE," goes,

> O Western wynd, when wilt thou blow
> And the small rain down shall rain
> O Christ that my love were in my arms
> And I in my bed again

What happened to the *tremendum* of the most surnatural song of the English Renaissance?

The brutal fact of the matter is that there simply does not exist even the vestige of a scientific approach to prosody. And it seems to be impossible to get any university to sponsor such research. The equipment is there—phonetics, phonology, philology, speech departments now have sound spectographs and all sorts of apparatus and the electronic boys have even more, not to mention Bell Telephone, whom I hereby invite to finance me in such a program. What little work has been done on poetry read aloud by sensitive, competent readers has revealed that the elements of speech that form the materials of the artist in words are far more complex than light and color, musical notes, or architectural, sculptural, and dance space, and that the prosodic analysis which we have inherited from the Greek grammarians of Alexandria and which they applied *after the fact,* often centuries after, had no real relevance to poetry in the English language and that the reading of poetry aloud by Englishmen and Americans differs drastically. Beyond those facts, which we knew already, we know practically nothing else. What is needed above all other things in poetry—of the sort academia could do anyway—is an exhaustive analysis of what happens, using all the armamentarium which lies there at hand to study sound. A sound spectograph picture of a line of poetry makes immediately apparent the tremendous complexity of the poetic effect. It is necessary to break this complicated graph down into its elements, degrees of accent, length and shape of syllables, pitch, and then the pattern of all these. These are only the elements that we have learned to call prosodic. Once we start analyzing it we will doubtless find others we never knew existed. Only in recent years has modern phonology discovered that French is a tonic language, like Swedish or Chinese, and that the tonic patterns not only strongly influence the meaning but that they vary with sex, class, occupational group, and of course geographical regions. It is the correct intonation of French that constitutes a "good accent." You can butcher the grammar and mispronounce the vowels but as long as you have something that sounds like a French intonation, the French will just think you are ignorant and from another part of France. Yet all this, seemingly so obvious, was discovered, in the scientific sense, only in the last generation.

The complexity of the material and its resistance to simple, home-made analysis is what makes most prosodic theory, whether of Hopkins, Bridges, Lanier, Yvor Winters, Olson, or whomever, seem cranky. It's the old story of the five blind men and the elephant. Olson at least is to be commended for trying, and for insisting that the ear, the breath, and the heart were better instruments of prosodic analysis than little hooks and lines and the patterns to be found in the back of a rhyming dictionary.

Those lyrics in the English language which survive in popular estimation as our most melodic—"Alysoun," "Westron Wynde," The Childe Ballads, Campion, Shakespeare, Waller, Burns, Blake, Landor, William Barnes, Tennyson, Thomas Moore—all have something in common which is very obvious when it is pointed out. They represent the survival of the fittest in the mouths of singers. Those rules that make a lyric singable they fulfill preëminently, but those rules do not come from prosodic theory, but from musical practice.

Revenons à nos moutons. Olson's masterwork was the *Maximus* poems, really one long personal revery like Zukofsky's *A,* Pound's *Cantos,* or Williams' *Paterson,* Lowenfels' *Some Deaths,* Thomas McGrath's *Letter to an Imaginary*

Friend. The long passages of *Maximus* are denser and less interesting than the most self-indulgent *Cantos.* Although he was preëminently a long-poem man, outsize in most everything he did, Olson is really best in shorter, highly compressed intimate poems.

In my opinion Gregory Corso is one of the best poets of his generation. He is completely a natural, like the painter, *le douanier* Rousseau. You either like him or you don't. There's not much you can say about him, except perhaps you could write a poem to him.

Allen Ginsberg dominates. He started out a good Columbia English major, a student of Jacques Barzun, Lionel Trilling, and Mark Van Doren, producing, while still an undergraduate, wryly humorous poems that owed much to the simpler pieces of William Carlos Williams. He came to San Francisco and met the poets there who had always considered his masters at Columbia, along with John Crowe Ransom and his friends, The General Staff of The Enemy. He learned fast. The libertarianism, personalism, internationalism of San Francisco exploded him. At the climacteric reading at the Six Gallery he blew up the crust of custom and overturned a complacent Establishment. For years afterwards They pretended he didn't exist, or called him a beatnik, but it is pretty hard to dismiss somebody who can fill the largest auditorium in any city he chooses to appear in—like Joan Baez, Bob Dylan, or the Beatles—and who has produced thousands of followers, in all the civilized and many uncivilized languages.

Ginsberg is one of the most traditionalist poets now living. His work is an almost perfect fulfillment of the long, Whitman, Populist, social revolutionary tradition in American poetry. In addition he is a latter-day *nabi,* one of those Hebrew prophets who came down out of the hills and cried "Woe! Woe! to the bloody city of Jerusalem!" in the streets. *Howl* resembles as much as anything the denunciatory poems of Jeremiah and Hosea. After Ginsberg, the fundamental American tradition, which was also the most international and the least provincial, was no longer on the defensive but moved over to the attack, and soon, as far as youthful audiences were concerned, the literary Establishment simply ceased to exist. It's not that Ginsberg is the greatest poet of the generation of the Fifties, although he is a very good one, it's that he had the most charismatic personality. The only poet in my time to compare with him in effect on audiences was Dylan Thomas, and Dylan Thomas was essentially a performer, whereas Ginsberg meant something of the greatest importance and so his effects have endured and permeated the whole society, and Thomas's have not.

Ginsberg is the only one of his immediate associates who outgrew the nihilistic alienation of the Beat Generation and moved on to the positive counter culture which developed in the Sixties. He was the spokesman of the lost youth of 1955 and he remained a spokesman of the youth who were struggling to found an alternative society in 1970. His influence is enormous, as great in India or Sweden or underground behind the Iron Curtain as it is in America.

All of these poets whom I have just been discussing are members of the world literary community in a way that no American poets before them except Whitman and to a lesser degree T. S. Eliot had ever been. They deprovincialized American poetry. Not only that, but the post-War Two world has not been very productive of good poets in Europe. French poetry for instance is probably at its lowest ebb in history. Only in Japan and the United States has there been anything like the flourishing poetic production

171

of the Twenties in Europe. So this group of poets is not only the most influential in the world today, but it is probably the best.

Conventional poetry has gone its way, now an essential part of the academic curriculum, "required for a B.A. for English Majors." Its proliferation has accompanied the educational and population explosions so that now there are almost as many professor poets on college campuses as there are new concrete buildings. The college poetry-reading circuit, begun so short a time ago in San Francisco, is now as widespread and more profitable than old-time vaudeville. The immense number of these people makes it difficult to see the wood for the trees and the trees for the shrubs. There is nothing wrong with this activity. It is good that, as in ancient China, postulants for an all-pervading bureaucracy should be taught to read and write a teachable kind of verse. Out of the immense mass some cream will rise to the top. After all Tu Fu, Li Po, Po Chu I, Su Tung Po, maybe the greatest non-dramatic, non-epic poets who ever lived, were products of such universal academic training in verse writing—and they were all bureaucrats. The problem when one is so close is simply one of gaining enough perspective to do a little sorting—who is best, better, and worst.

The process that led to the development of a full-blown, official, bureaucratic, and academic American literature began during the Second War when hundreds of writers were employed at desk jobs in the armed services or their appanages. People who had dreamed of martyrdom and learned a set of exercises and given up cigarettes so they'd keep fit in prison or concentration camps changed their minds and crowded into the swivel chairs in Washington

172

offices. After the war was safely over many of them transfered to the OSS, predecessor of the CIA, and took interesting trips abroad to teach the Germans and Italians and French the great truths of democracy and free enterprise. Before the onset of the Cold War many of these people were radicals in art or politics or both. Some of them were even Communists, but once relations between Russia and the United States cooled, these were ruthlessly purged.

Adapting the name of the independent League for Cultural Freedom founded by Diego Rivera, André Breton, and a number of American Surrealists and radicals at the time of the Moscow Trials, a Congress for Cultural Freedom was called in Berlin under the auspices of the American State Department, the CIA, and Military Intelligence. A chain of magazines was established, some of them already in existence, of which the best known came to be: *Encounter* in England, *The Partisan Review* in the United States, *Preuves* in France, *Der Monat* in Germany, all with very prestigious panels of editors, some of them innocents. At the same time what before the war would have seemed to be enormous sums of money were made available for what the Russians called "American cultural imperialism" —actually, state-subsidized intercultural relations no different from their own.

In Japan, India, Italy where Ignazio Silone was an editor, and other countries, these ventures failed of their purpose, aroused antagonism, and were isolated. *Der Monat* and *Encounter,* the best edited, became very influential indeed, especially the former, which was edited with a mocking disregard for American literary officialdom and its policy. Direct connections between the CIA and the American literary establishment have been difficult to prove

173

but magazines like *The Partisan Review*, the *Kenyon*, the *Hudson* reviews, and *Commentary* have at least been voluntary members of the same school of letters.

Given the assumption of a nation state, threatened by another nation state, there is nothing wrong with this, and there is the additional factor that, although it is practically impossible to get money out of the United States Congress for cultural activities of any significance, there is no difficulty whatever in obtaining unlimited funds for espionage and the secret police. To a certain extent CIA sponsorship was simply a device to outwit militantly mindless politicians.

Nevertheless, cultural freedom or no, twenty years of this program led to a thorough-going officialization of American writers, artists, musicians, scholars, and all other culture-bearers who were willing to lend themselves to it. If the essence of the art of this industrial, financial epoch is its alienation, then the American bureaucracy managed to make a great deal of American art very inartistic. What was worse is that this new Establishment did not just pretend; it literally did not know that anything or anybody else existed.

Sung and T'ang China would indicate that a Mandarin literature can perhaps become one of the highest of which mankind is capable, but certainly from the end of the Second War on, American literature, but especially American poetry, divides increasingly into Mandarin and non-Mandarin. If this is not understood, the literary currents of a whole generation are not comprehensible.

Beginning before the war with poets like Delmore Schwartz, Elizabeth Bishop, Jean Garrigue, the Establishment began to develop its own "advanced writers"; the rear-guard's avant-garde, so to speak, and during and after

174

the war added some very significant poets indeed—John Berryman, Robert Lowell, Theodore Roethke, Richard Wilbur, amongst others. Of these Robert Lowell is probably the best. A kind of Yankee Allen Tate, he actually wrote an answer, *For the Union Dead,* to Tate's "Elegy for the Confederate Dead." Lowell is genuinely, by nature and by inheritance, a true Protestant, metaphysical, Baroque poet. His conflicts and dilemmas are those of Herman Melville and Emily Dickinson and his language is rooted in spiritual ancestors like George Chapman and Du Bartas—he is certainly a better poet than the latter. Overlying religious and philosophical issues was a cloud of storms of personal and pyschological conflicts which give his poetry its poignant immediacy. He is certainly the most important poet of his group.

The poetry of Theodore Roethke could easily be described in the same terms but it would be an inaccurate description because Roethke is in every way a slighter thinker than Lowell and a slighter technician. Roethke's virtues are almost purely personal and his best poems are about his childhood and youth, about a girl student killed falling from a horse, and other simple fragments of autobiography. The same could have been said of John Berryman except that Berryman has a very complex personality, if not a complex intellect, and his ability to describe the adventures of that personality make him one of the best of the so-called "confessional" poets.

Richard Wilbur is almost exactly the opposite of these three poets. At least as he presents it in his poetry, life does not offer insoluable problems, nor are good verses hard to write. The others run the danger of turgidity or impenetrable privacy. Wilbur's danger is facility. It is interesting that he has found it congenial to translate French verse of the seventeenth and eighteenth centuries which has the same virtues and the same faults as his own.

Not all poets who write what the Black Mountain or San Francisco groups would dismiss as conventional verse are members of the Establishment. If W. S. Merwin is established, and he is, it is on his own terms.

Merwin is a more ambitious poet than Richard Wilbur. However colloquial and domestic, the poem always has mythic scope, less subjective, more, not social, but anthropological than Robert Lowell, but like him in Melville's tradition of overturned Puritanism, Merwin shares a literal resemblance to Melville in his intense feeling for the specific under a storm of language. Little contemporary poetry is as dramatic as his, full of different people in different relationships to each other, not a common habit of serious American poetry. Each of Merwin's books has been a step from that academic fashion of imitation Baroque, which he handled with great skill, toward ever greater modesty and immediacy of utterance.

Then comes a succession of poets who have evolved like Merwin—W. D. Snodgrass, James Wright, Robert Bly, Louis Simpson, Galway Kinnell. Most publish in *The Sixties* and *The Seventies* edited by Robert Bly; most started in the Middle West. Today a younger contingent, inheritors of this group, might be called "The Reformed Neo-Academics." Most impressive are Anne Sexton, Tim Reynolds, Adrienne Rich, Thom Gunn, and A. R. Ammons. Coming up behind them are William Knott (Saint Geraud), and Robert Kelly. Their characteristics are acid wit, a relaxed use of conventional form, and a return to intimate speech in the first person that the misleading snobbery of T. S. Eliot had made unfashionable for thirty years.

William Knott, Jerome Rothenberg, and Robert Kelly could hardly be called academic poets, for they share with the younger members of the San Francisco and Black Mountain groups and Gary Snyder and Philip Whalen a new, international, so-called modernist idiom. Rothenberg, a learned and highly skilled poet, also shares with Snyder and Whalen a profound understanding of the poetry of pre-literate people and of non-Western European life attitudes.

Snyder is probably the most influential—on the young— poet of his generation—influential as a poet on new poets, that is. Ginsberg is still the charismatic leader. Snyder is the best informed, most thoughtful, and most articulate of his colleagues. He has a perfectly clear, carefully thought out life philosophy in which the ecological concept of all life as community, the mutual aid of Kropotkin, the Bud-dhist love and respect for all sentient creatures, and the primitive animist's organic identification with living things are merged into a coherent and readily negotiable pattern, completely relevant to the contemporary situation, a new ethic, a new esthetic, a new life style which is emerging amongst artists, writers, musicians, and the youth for whom they speak as Western Civilization enters its period of final breakdown. Snyder is also an accomplished technician who has learned from the poetry of several languages and who has developed a sure and flexible style capable of handling any material he wishes.

The same words could apply to his friend, Philip Whalen, except that Whalen, having lived in Japan now for a good many years, and having published only in limited or ex-pensive editions, is simply not well enough known. Twenty years before ecology became a fashionable evasion, Snyder and Whalen, then students at Reed College, were talking about the ecological revolution and the community of love and learning from the mountains and rivers and the Indians of the Northwest and studying Buddhism and Hinduism. Theirs is a kind of ecological esthetics. They are always aware that the poem is the nexus of the biota, the knot of macrocosm and microcosm, a jewel in Shiva's necklace.

A poem is a perspective on a person and a person is a totalized perspective on all other sentient beings. Something very like this is going to be the philosophy and the art, the poetry, of the future if there is a future. Although they both write of similar subjects with a similar philosophy in a superficially similar style, it would be a great mistake to confuse Snyder and Whalen. The difference is a difference of sensibility and in poetry that is all the difference that matters. Whalen sees the world as profoundly comic—a divine comedy. Snyder's vision is not tragic in the superficial sense but is certainly elegiac, more akin to the great elegiac poets of Sung China.

With Snyder, Whalen, Rothenberg, Bill Knott, Leonard Cohen, we are already deep into the counter culture, the alternative society which has developed from the schism in the soul and the secession of the elites as Western Civilization came to an end after the Second War, a process enormously accelerated by the Vietnam War which split society, not just in America but in the whole Western world, with an unbridgeable schism. Poetry and music have been the two pivots of the counter culture and their proliferation has been immense. With the population explosion and the education explosion and the affluent society the arts have become democratized. It seems as though everybody under thirty writes poetry, plays the guitar and writes songs for it, paints psychedelic pictures, makes junk sculpture, and, if the money is available, makes films.

Ever since the Second War the most significant poetry

178

in France has been sung. *Café chantant* singers like Georges Brassens and Anne Sylvestre are incomparably better poets than the post-war crop of French who write only for print and who bear an unfortunate resemblance to the duller poets of the American academy. Lyrics by Bob Dylan, Donovan, Lennon and McCartney, Leonard Cohen, Joni Mitchell, and Judy Collins rank with best poetry in English of their generation and they have thousands of imitators and disciples.

All the papers of the underground press print poetry and there are countless little magazines and broadsides, some of them turned out on a home mimeograph with no circulation beyond a group of friends, others printed on fine presses, others with a circulation of several thousand, and there are many presses turning out books and booklets for the counter culture. The pioneer was Ferlinghetti's City Lights Press with its Pocket Poetry series. One of the finest and most comprehensive in its selection of poets is the Black Sparrow Press in Los Angeles, a large, homogenized, smogbound area in the lower left hand corner of the United States hitherto considered cultural desert. Many of the large trade publishing houses and several university presses now have poetry series with several titles a year. These tend to be conventional and largely confined to academic poets but once in a while somebody new and exciting slips by. Columbia University Press no sooner started its series than they came up with a genuinely original poet, Joseph Ceravolo. There has been a revival of Surrealism, both of poetry written in the style of the classic Surrealists, especially Robert Desnos, and young poets in direct communication with the new, intensely political, or rather anti-political young anarchist Surrealists in France. The best I know is Sotere Torregian. American poets have also taken part in

179

the worldwide revival of concrete poetry begun so long ago in pre-War One Russia and their work has been amongst the extremely interesting.

Traditionally American poetry has been most prudish except for that of the bohemian underworld. In his day even Conrad Aiken was frowned upon because he dealt very chastely with erotic subjects. Today erotic poetry is common, Elizabeth Sargent is very popular, and Lenore Kandel's *The Love Book* was a worldwide bestseller. Now there are hundreds like it. This has been a time of wholesale translation, everything from Homer, Gilgamesh, and the Norse sagas to the work of German Expressionists and Russian Futurists has been retranslated. Hundreds of poets who have never been translated before are now available in English versions. There are anthologies of classic and modern poetry of most of the civilized languages and excellent collections of preliterate song.